INTRODUCING
ISSUES WITH
OPPOSING
VIEWPOINTS®

The
Environment

Other books in the Introducing Issues
with Opposing Viewpoints series:

AIDS
Alcohol
Animal Rights
Civil Liberties
Cloning
The Death Penalty
Energy Alternatives
Gangs
Gay Marriage
Genetic Engineering
Islam
Smoking
Terrorism
UFOs

INTRODUCING
ISSUES WITH
OPPOSING
VIEWPOINTS®

The
Environment

Andrea C. Nakaya, *Book Editor*

Bonnie Szumski, *Publisher, Series Editor*
Helen Cothran, *Managing Editor*

GREENHAVEN PRESS
An imprint of Thomson Gale, a part of The Thomson Corporation

THOMSON
GALE

Detroit • New York • San Francisco • San Diego • New Haven, Conn. • Waterville, Maine • London • Munich

LIBRARY OF CONGRESS CATALOGING-IN-PUBLICATION DATA

The environment / Andrea C. Nakaya, book editor.
    p. cm. — (Introducing issues with opposing viewpoints)
    Includes bibliographical references and index.
    ISBN 0-7377-3459-0 (lib. bdg. : alk. paper)
    1. United States—Environmental conditions. 2. Environment policy—United States.
    3. Environmental ethics—United States. I. Nakaya, Andrea C., 1976– II. Series.
    GE150.E57 2006
    333.72—dc22

                                                                    2005056281

Printed in the United States of America

Contents

Chapter 3: What Should America's Environmental Policies Be?

Foreword

Indulging in a wide spectrum of ideas, beliefs, and perspectives is a critical cornerstone of democracy. After all, it is often debates over differences of opinion, such as whether to legalize abortion, how to treat prisoners, or when to enact the death penalty, that shape our society and drive it forward. Such diversity of thought is frequently regarded as the hallmark of a healthy and civilized culture. As the Reverend Clifford Schutjer of the First Congregational Church in Mansfield, Ohio, declared in a 2001 sermon, "Surrounding oneself with only like-minded people, restricting what we listen to or read only to what we find agreeable is irresponsible. Refusing to entertain doubts once we make up our minds is a subtle but deadly form of arrogance." With this advice in mind, Introducing Issues with Opposing Viewpoints books aim to open readers' minds to the critically divergent views that comprise our world's most important debates.

Introducing Issues with Opposing Viewpoints simplifies for students the enormous and often overwhelming mass of material now available via print and electronic media. Collected in every volume is an array of opinions that captures the essence of a particular controversy or topic. Introducing Issues with Opposing Viewpoints books embody the spirit of nineteenth-century journalist Charles A. Dana's axiom: "Fight for your opinions, but do not believe that they contain the whole truth, or the only truth." Absorbing such contrasting opinions teaches students to analyze the strength of an argument and compare it to its opposition. From this process readers can inform and strengthen their own opinions, or be exposed to new information that will change their minds. Introducing Issues with Opposing Viewpoints is a mosaic of different voices. The authors are statesmen, pundits, academics, journalists, corporations, and ordinary people who have felt compelled to share their experiences and ideas in a public forum. Their words have been collected from newspapers, journals, books, speeches, interviews, and the Internet, the fastest growing body of opinionated material in the world.

Introducing Issues with Opposing Viewpoints shares many of the well-known features of its critically acclaimed parent series, Opposing Viewpoints. The articles are presented in a pro/con format, allowing readers to absorb divergent perspectives side by side. Active reading questions preface each viewpoint, requiring the student to approach the material thoughtfully and carefully. Useful charts, graphs, and cartoons supplement each article. A thorough introduction provides readers with crucial background on an issue. An annotated bibliography points the reader toward articles, books, and Web sites that contain additional information on the topic. An appendix of organizations to contact contains a wide variety of charities, nonprofit organizations, political groups, and private enterprises that each hold a position on the issue at hand. Finally, a comprehensive index allows readers to locate content quickly and efficiently.

Introducing Issues with Opposing Viewpoints is also significantly different from Opposing Viewpoints. As the series title implies, its presentation will help introduce students to the concept of opposing viewpoints, and learn to use this material to aid in critical writing and debate. The series' four-color, accessible format makes the books attractive and inviting to readers of all levels. In addition, each viewpoint has been carefully edited to maximize a reader's understanding of the content. Short but thorough viewpoints capture the essence of an argument. A substantial, thought-provoking essay question placed at the end of each viewpoint asks the student to further investigate the issues raised in the viewpoint, compare and contrast two authors' arguments, or consider how one might go about forming an opinion on the topic at hand. Each viewpoint contains sidebars that include at-a-glance information and handy statistics. A Facts About section located in the back of the book further supplies students with relevant facts and figures.

Following in the tradition of the Opposing Viewpoints series, Greenhaven Press continues to provide readers with invaluable exposure to the controversial issues that shape our world. As John Stuart Mill once wrote: "The only way in which a human being can make some approach to knowing the whole of a subject is by hearing what can be said about it by persons of every variety of opinion and studying all modes in which it can be looked at by every character of mind. No wise man ever acquired his wisdom in any mode but this." It is to this principle that Introducing Issues with Opposing Viewpoints books are dedicated.

Introduction

"[Communities] must integrate environmental stewardship, economic development and the well-being of all people—not just for today but for countless generations to come."

—International Institute for Sustainable Development

I
n the early 1990s a small bird called the northern spotted owl was the cause of an environmental controversy in the United States. Studies showed that the owl, which lives in forests in the Pacific Northwest, was in danger of extinction. The U.S. Fish and Wildlife Service thus listed the bird as threatened under the Endangered Species Act, meaning that both the owl and its habitat must be protected. The owl's habitat, however, was also an important source of wood for the lumber industry, which provided thousands of jobs to people in that area. A fierce battle ensued over which was more deserving of protection: the forests that the owl lived in, or the livelihoods of thousands of lumber workers.

As the case of the spotted owl illustrates, protecting the environment—one necessity of life—often conflicts with industry, jobs, and other necessities of life. This means that society must constantly decide how to balance environmental conservation with other interests such as economic development and financial well-being. As this book shows, there are varying ideas about how to achieve this balance.

It is widely understood that on a very basic level, humans need a healthy environment to survive and flourish. People need clean air to breathe and unpolluted food and water to fuel their bodies. They also need the environment to be healthy enough so that its many resources—such as food or raw materials for building—can be used by humans to further society. But the importance of the environment also goes beyond basic survival and a productive society. Nature is a rich source of enjoyment and recreation; many can attest to the joy felt from seeing a beautiful view or swimming in a crystal-clear lake. Nick Dusic, science policy manager at the British Ecological Society, explains the link between a healthy human population and a healthy environment: "The services that ecosystems provide are fundamental to our well-being," says Dusic.

> When we eat food, drink a glass of water or enjoy a walk in the woods, we are enjoying the things our ecosystems do for us. . . . When we over-exploit fish stocks, our economy grows more slowly than it otherwise would, due to the loss of the fishing industry. When we log upland forests, we are less secure due to the increased risk of flooding. When we pollute freshwater ecosystems, we are less healthy due to poor water quality.

Therefore, communities have an interest in preserving the health of their environment for their own survival.

Yet in many instances, environmental preservation comes into conflict with economic growth and financial well-being, which are also integral to a healthy society. Modern industries often rapidly use up natural resources or produce harmful by-products as they manufac-

Air pollution is a growing problem in many American cities. Here, pollutants from a factory smokestack pour into the atmosphere.

Clean beaches, like Waikiki Beach in Honolulu, Hawaii, are just one of the many benefits of maintaining a healthy environment.

ture items. Yet these industries are vital to the creation of much-needed products, jobs, and other necessities of modern society. For example, forests in the Pacific Northwest contain lumber, a resource that supports a vast network of jobs, including logging and the manufacture of wood products. If regulation of logging is too strict, it will hamper this industry's ability to grow economically. In such a case environmental protection must be weighed against the threat it poses to the well-being of society. As the president of the Northwest Forestry Association argued during the spotted owl controversy, the protection of business is at times more important than the protection of nature. "To devastate a regional economy over the spotted owl seems absurd," he said.

To placate those holding such widely differing views on the environment, society attempts to find a compromise. After all, everyone has some interest in environmental protection, and everyone has some interest in the preservation of business and economic well-being. As author

Although logging provides a valuable natural resource and promotes job growth, the loss of forests can lead to flooding and other environmental threats.

John Roush puts it, "No one—not even the most dedicated environmentalist—wants to go without food, shelter, and a livelihood," and "no one—not even the most dedicated industrialist or miner—wants to go without clean air and water and green places." However there is rarely agreement on where that compromise lies. Researchers Bruce D. Cowen and Kathryn R. Braithwaite talk about the process of finding a balance, likening it to an "environmental pendulum." According to them, sometimes the pendulum swings in favor of business, and sometimes it swings in favor of the environment. They conclude, however, that "although a formidable challenge, environmental equilibrium can be achieved."

The actions society should take to find the balance between protecting the natural world and encouraging economic growth and development is a source of continual debate. This controversy is explored further in *Introducing Issues with Opposing Viewpoints: The Environment*, as the authors offer various arguments on the environmental issues facing society today.

Chapter 1

Is There an Environmental Crisis?

The United States produces billions of tons of trash every year.

The United States Faces an Environmental Crisis

J. William Gibson

"Toxic contamination threatens the health of the country."

In the following viewpoint J. William Gibson argues that cheap consumer goods have created widespread pollution in the United States. As a result, he believes the country faces an environmental crisis. He warns that both businesses and individuals need to stop acting solely for profit and convenience. Unless the country starts caring for the environment, America's natural resources will be completely destroyed, he says. Gibson is a professor of sociology at California State University, Long Beach.

AS YOU READ, CONSIDER THE FOLLOWING QUESTIONS:
1. According to the author, what are the hidden costs of "cheap" coal-fired electricity?
2. Why are many consumers in denial about environmental threats, according to Gibson?
3. In the author's opinion, what effect does buying organic food have on the green market?

In January [2004] the Los Angeles Department of Water and Power [DWP] announced plans to increase its investment in coal-fired electrical generating plants in southern Utah. Electricity produced by coal is cheap—one-tenth the cost of solar energy—which means it is quite profitable. And because surplus revenue from the DWP makes up 7% of the cash-strapped city of L.A.'s general fund, increasing the output of lucrative coal plants seems like a rational move.

But here's the problem. Over the last few years, numerous studies have found that it is no longer safe to eat much swordfish, marlin, tuna and many other ocean fish because of mercury contamination. Mercury seriously harms human nervous systems, especially those of unborn babies and young children. And 40% of the airborne mercury particles that end up polluting ecosystems and accumulating in animals and humans come from coal-fired electrical generating plants.

Coal-mining operations around the world consume millions of gallons of water each year as part of the process to extract the fuel source from the earth.

When the DWP calls coal-fired electricity "cheap," its calculations don't include damage to the fishing industry. They don't take into account the lifetime medical costs incurred by families of children hurt by mercury or the vast environmental damage inflicted by coal mining. They don't consider the blighted landscape left behind or the aquifer depletion that results from millions of gallons of scarce water diverted for use in coal slurries. There's also the coal haze from the generating plants that despoils the skies and contributes to global warming and its potentially disastrous climatic changes.

A Risk Society

The coal example is by no means exceptional, but part of an overall pattern of what sociologists call "risk society." Around World War II, industrial production became both more technologically sophisticated and much larger in scale. But the new technologies that promised greater

"I FIND THE STONE AGE, THE BRONZE AGE, THE IRON AGE, THE USE-IT-AND-THROW-IT-AWAY AGE..."

Alexander. © by Copley News Service. Reproduced by permission.

profits for business and cheaper goods for consumers also created widespread risks—and science, which was indispensable in developing these new technologies, most often ignored potential problems. "In the risk society," wrote sociologist Ulrich Beck, " . . . unknown and unintended consequences come to be a dominant force in history and society."

Our risk society has brought us nuclear plants that can generate vast amounts of electricity but also create wastes that remain lethal for hundreds of thousands of years. Cars and trucks have become bigger and faster, but their exhausts have caused cancer clusters along major freeways and unleashed smog that has choked major cities. Industrialized agriculture has produced mountains of cheap food but requires pesticides and herbicides that can cause cancer or impair reproduction in animals and humans. Powerful solvents can clean industrial machines like a charm but include highly toxic carcinogens that have made their way into the groundwater. A 108-million-gallon underground plume of water polluted with the chemical compound chromium 6 is within 125 feet of the Colorado River, the principal water source for 18 million Southern California residents.

FAST FACT

According to a 2005 report by *Mother Earth News*, the United States generates 12 billion tons of trash every year.

In Denial

We have come to accept risk society as inevitable. Part of this acceptance comes from the way industry separates products from the production process. When we buy food in the grocery store, we don't see how it was sprayed in the field. When we turn on lights in L.A., we don't see the plants and coal mines that generated the power. Moreover, the news we receive is highly fragmented. Stories about new electrical plants in Utah rarely mention mercury contamination in fish, nor do stories about contaminated fish often mention power plants. Only those paying careful attention make the connections. Another part of the problem is that we are reluctant to question science, which has such prestige that people rarely stop to question who is funding research and whether that could compromise findings.

Volunteers clean up a beach after an oil spill. Such spills are a consequence of shipping oil in large tankers around the world.

Ultimately, we are all in denial. Industry wants to deny responsibility for pollutants because at the very minimum, eliminating them requires spending money. And consumers are in denial because in some cases, ending toxic wastes might mean that popular products would have to be discontinued. Politicians know that creating and enforcing government regulations to radically restrict pollution would evoke industry opposition and political retaliation.

Breaking the Pattern

Living in a risk society is not unavoidable. But to change things, we need to break through all these forms of denial and recognize that toxic contamination threatens the health of the country—and ultimately threatens our national security. The government can act to limit risk, as when it banned [the pesticide] DDT, but politicians are unlikely to take action without public pressure. Scientists not connected with industry must be involved in evaluating the dangers of various products and production processes, which happens with the Food and Drug Administration on drug licensing. Pollution can be aggressively targeted and violators prosecuted, but first the government has to focus on the big picture.

Changing investment practices can also help. Cities, states and major corporations all have massive pension funds that could be directed to invest only in corporations utilizing clean technologies. Last month [February 2004] California Treasurer Phil Angelides made just such a proposal, calling for public employee pension funds to invest $1 billion in environmentally responsible businesses.

And although saying that individuals can make a difference by changing what they buy seems almost naive, over time it can produce results. It's deeply threatening, often inconvenient and sometimes costly to take responsibility for what we buy and its effects upon the environment. But enough people doing so has an effect. Organic food had its origins in the '60s counterculture. Now it's in every grocery store, and people with absolutely no hippie blood in them swear by it. If people change what they buy, the green market won't just be a niche market but will alter how most goods are made.

Most important, the elimination of risk society requires breaking the pattern of responding to toxic pollution and wastes only after major disasters or the news that some common activity, like eating fresh fish, is now a major health risk. What's needed instead are the will and awareness to connect all the dots—politics, corporate technologies, personal consumption—and think about our legacy to future generations. We owe them a world that's alive and well, not a dangerous, depleted wasteland.

EVALUATING THE AUTHORS' ARGUMENTS:

In the viewpoint you just read, J. William Gibson warns that America is approaching an environmental crisis. In the next viewpoint, Alex A. Avery and Dennis T. Avery contend that reports about America's environmental problems have been greatly exaggerated. In your opinion, which of the two viewpoints makes the most persuasive argument? Explain.

The U.S. Environmental Crisis Has Been Exaggerated

"The public is too often given only one-sided, simplistic, pessimistic versions of environmental realities."

Alex A. Avery and Dennis T. Avery

The U.S. media and regulatory agencies report bad news about the environment and ignore good news, maintain Alex A. Avery and Dennis T. Avery in the following viewpoint. As a result, the authors argue, the public is led to believe that America's environment is in crisis. This is not accurate, the authors assert. They believe that regulatory agencies and the media focus only on bad news in order to gain money and power. Alex A. Avery is director of research and education at the Hudson Institute's Center for Global Food Issues. Dennis T. Avery is director of the center.

AS YOU READ, CONSIDER THE FOLLOWING QUESTIONS:

1. Why do Northwest salmon numbers naturally increase and decrease, according to the authors?
2. According to Avery and Avery, how much media attention did the Bond report on global warming receive?
3. How does bad news about the environment benefit regulatory agencies, in the authors' opinion?

Alex A. Avery and Dennis T. Avery, "Intellectual Polluters," *American Outlook,* vol. 1, Fall 2003, pp. 32–36. Copyright © 2003 by the Hudson Institute in Indianapolis. Reproduced by permission.

M uch good news about contentious environmental issues is regularly kept quiet by regulatory agencies, activist groups, and the media. Why this is so is the question we have continually asked ourselves after closely examining the most recent scientific research behind . . . important contemporary environmental debates in the United States. . . .

The good news is that there is plenty of good news. The bad news is that hardly anyone is reporting or discussing it, so that the public continues to believe in environmental crises that are nonexistent. Because such crises often result in new laws, policies, and regulations—and thus have widespread and lasting effects on our communities and economy—we ignore the blackout on good news at our peril.

Lies About Northwest Salmon

In August of this year [2003], President [George W.] Bush visited the Ice Harbor power dam on the Snake River to celebrate the strong Northwest

President Bush speaks at the Ice Harbor power dam in Washington, claiming that strong salmon runs in recent years are evidence of a healthy environment.

salmon runs of the last two years. Salmon numbers in the Columbia River basin have lately been the highest in four decades. Salmon fishermen in northern California celebrated the Fourth of July (and record salmon hauls) by giving their fellow citizens free salmon. . . .

The *Washington Post* reported on August 20, 2003, "Everyone agrees that the primary reason for the recent abundance of salmon is a dramatic improvement in ocean conditions." That is a lie by omission.

Because salmon run in twenty-five year cycles, it is difficult to make conclusions about their population on a year-to-year basis.

The key fact to remember about Northwest salmon is that they migrate in a twenty-five-year cycle. . . . For twenty-five years at a time, the Pacific currents carry lots of salmon food (bait fish) to the coasts of Washington, Oregon, and Northern California, and the salmon thrive there. Meanwhile, the salmon to the north in the Gulf of Alaska go hungry and decline. Then, for the next twenty-five years, the fish food goes up to Alaska, and the salmon in the Columbia River basin appear to be going extinct. Nature allows each of the two fisheries to thrive alternately, but never simultaneously.

Fishery journals going back at least to 1915 have documented this pattern, which scientists call "co-variance." The salmon catch data for Oregon show one of the clearest such patterns to be found in nature. You can almost set your calendar by the salmon runs; the recent downtrend in Columbia River salmon numbers started in 1977. . . .

Nevertheless, when the salmon runs began—predictably—to improve two years ago, the *Portland Oregonian* pioneered the explanation of "improved ocean conditions" later cited by the *Washington Post*. The newspapers have not identified any specific ocean conditions that have changed. This omission has allowed them to avoid telling their readers that they failed to explain the salmon cycle in 1977, when the population decline began and the activists commenced to wail about "salmon extinction" and demanding the shutdown of commercial fishing, logging, and farming in the region. It is difficult to believe that none of the *Oregonian*'s readers have pointed out the cycle phenomenon to the editors, as some of the region's fishermen have lived through two or even three of the twenty-five-year cycles. It seems likely that the newspaper has deliberately suppressed this information. . . .

Scare Scenario

On November 16, 2001, the journal *Science* published an elegant research report, done by unimpeachable scientists, recounting the earth's temperature history for the past 12,000 years. The report directly linked Earth's changing climate to the variable behavior of the sun. Dr. Gerard Bond and a team from the Lamont-Doherty Earth Observatory in Palisades, New York (and affiliated with Columbia University) compiled the report. . . .

The research implies that global warming has nothing to do with the activities of mankind. This scientific bombshell was almost totally ignored by the media, despite the favorable comments in *Science,* which journalists watch carefully for news. In fact, an Internet search revealed that not a single publication other than *Science* and *American Outlook* reported the Bond research.

Contrast this with the massive media play given to a scary "abrupt climate cooling" scenario published in 2002 by Dr. Robert Gagosian, director of the Woods Hole Oceanographic Institute in Massachusetts. Gagosian speculated that too much warming—releasing too much fresh water from glaciers—might overwhelm the Gulf Stream, which carries warm tropical water north and moderates the temperatures in the North Atlantic and Europe. He predicted that the Northeastern United States might chill by as much as 10 degrees Fahrenheit, freezing our rivers and forcing wholesale changes in farming and fishing, even as our energy costs soared exponentially. "We're walking toward a cliff blindfolded," said Gagosian—who then demanded that the world spend more money on marine research to match the scare-driven spending on atmospheric climate research to combat global warming.

Gagosian was merely offering a theory, of course—and making an obviously self-interested pitch for research dollars. But his scare scenario was widely published, in both *Science* and *Nature,* and in prominent newspapers such as the *Boston Globe,* the *Christian Science Monitor,* the *Philadelphia Inquirer,* and Canada's *National Post.* It was also widely publicized on the Internet sites of the World Economic Forum, the Cambridge Conference, Sustainable Minnesota, and the University of Georgia.

Both the Bond and Gagosian stories came from reputable research institutions. One reported actual historical facts that should ease our fears. It remains virtually ignored. The Gagosian scare offered an

Optimism About the Environment

A 2005 Gallup poll indicates that a majority of Americans are optimistic that environmental problems will be well under control in twenty years.

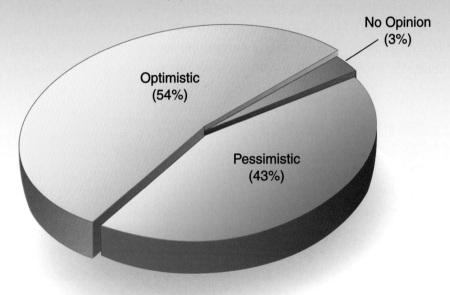

No Opinion (3%)

Optimistic (54%)

Pessimistic (43%)

Source: Gallup poll, 2005.

undocumented theoretical horror, and was spun instantly and broadly across the world. . . .

Watchdogs—or Attack Dogs?

These . . . instances amply demonstrate that the public is too often given only one-sided, simplistic, pessimistic versions of environmental realities by the news media and even by our government agencies and researchers.

The reasons why are fairly simple and obvious: money and power. For the news media, bad news sells. It doesn't take a genius to know that a newspaper with a scary headline will sell far more copies than the paper declaring, "Nothing Bad Happened Yesterday, Tomorrow Looks Great!" It is a basic fact of human nature.

For our regulatory watchdog agencies, bad news means huge increases in research and staff funding. The amount of dollars spent on climate change research and watchdogging is billions higher today than before the threat of human-caused climate change was postulated. Likewise for environmental groups, whose donations and memberships skyrocket with these crisis campaigns. . . .

Any decent society will have a healthy level of scientific disagreement and discourse. In fact, vigorous debate is critical for the progress of science. But that is exactly the point: true scientific debates are being stymied in the media and within our regulatory agencies.

EVALUATING THE AUTHORS' ARGUMENTS:

List three different examples or statistics that Alex A. Avery and Dennis T. Avery use to support their contention that bad news about the environment has been exaggerated. Which of these do you find the most convincing? Why?

Viewpoint
3

Species Extinction Is a Serious Problem

Janet Larsen

"We now are moving toward another mass extinction."

In the following viewpoint Janet Larsen warns that the world is headed for mass extinction. Humans have transformed the environment, harmed plants and animals, and driven large numbers of species to extinction, says Larsen. She urges humans to act to prevent an extinction crisis. Larsen is a research associate at the Earth Policy Institute, an organization dedicated to creating an environmentally sustainable economy.

AS YOU READ, CONSIDER THE FOLLOWING QUESTIONS:

1. As argued by the author, compared to the extinction rate of the past 60 million years, how much faster is the current extinction rate?
2. What is the greatest threat to the world's living creatures, in Larsen's opinion?
3. According to the author, what percentage of species could be wiped out by climate change?

Almost 440,000,000 years ago, some 85% of marine animal species were wiped out in the Earth's first known mass extinction. Roughly 73,000,000 years later, large quantities of fish and 70% of marine invertebrates perished in a second major extinction event. Then, about 245,000,000 years ago, up to 95% of all animals were lost in what is thought to be the worst extinction in history. Approximately 37,000,000 years hence, yet another mass extinction took a toll primarily on sea creatures, but also some land animals. Finally, 65,000,000 years ago, three-quarters of all species—including the dinosaurs—were eliminated.

Among the possible causes of these mass extinctions were volcanic eruptions, falling meteorites, and changing climate. After each extinction, it took upwards of 10,000,000 years for biological richness to recover. Yet, once a species is gone, it is gone for good.

Another Mass Extinction

The consensus among biologists is that we now are moving toward another mass extinction that could rival the past big five. This one is

Some scientists fear the planet is moving toward another mass extinction, similar to the event 65 million years ago (pictured in this illustration) that wiped out dinosaurs and thousands of other species.

A section of Brazilian rain forest burns after being cleared by loggers. Rain forests are home to some of the world's most diverse plant and animal populations.

unique, however, in that it is largely caused by the activities of a single species. It is the sole mass extinction that humans will witness first-hand—and not just as innocent bystanders.

While scientists are not sure how many species inhabit the planet today, their estimates top 10,000,000. Each year, though, thousands of species, ranging from the smallest microorganisms to larger mammals, are lost forever. Some disappear even before we know of their existence.

The average extinction rate today is up to 10,000 times faster than the rate that has prevailed over the past 60,000,000 years. Throughout most of geological history, new species evolved faster than existing species disappeared, thus continuously increasing the planet's biological diversity. Now, evolution is falling behind.

Disappearing Species

Only a small fraction of the world's plant species has been studied in detail, but as many as half are threatened with extinction. South and Central America, Central and West Africa, and Southeast Asia—all home to diverse tropical forests—are losing plants most rapidly. Moreover, nearly 5,500 animal species are known to be threatened with extinction. The International Union for Conservation of Nature and Natural Resources–World Conservation Union's 2003 Red List survey of the world's flora

Conservation Status of Birds

Status	Total (number)	Share (percent)
Not currently threatened	7,633	80
Nearing threatened status	875	9
Threatened—vulnerable to extinction	704	7
Threatened—in immediate danger of extinction	403	4

Some 20% of all bird species are now under threat of extinction.

Source: New Internationalist, www.newint.org, March 2002.

and fauna shows that almost one in every four mammals and one in eight birds are threatened with extinction within the next several decades.

Of 1,130 threatened mammals, 16% are critically endangered—the highest threat level. This means that 184 of their species have suffered extreme and rapid reduction in population or habitat and may not survive the decade. Their remaining numbers range from under a few hundred to, at most, a few thousand. For birds, 182 of the 1,194 threatened species are critically endangered.

Although the status of most of the world's mammals and birds is fairly well-documented, we know relatively little about the rest of the world's fauna. A mere five percent of fish, six percent of reptiles, and seven percent of amphibians have been evaluated. Of those studied, at least 750 fish species, 290 reptiles, and 150 amphibians are at risk. Worrisome signs—like the mysterious disappearance of entire amphibian populations and fishermen's nets that come up empty more frequently—reveal that there may be more species in trouble. Of invertebrates, including insects, mollusks, and crustaceans, we know the least—but what is known is far from reassuring.

The Effect of Humans

At the advent of agriculture some 11,000 years ago, the world was home to 6,000,000 people. Since then, our ranks have grown a thousandfold. Yet, the increase in our numbers has come at the expense of many other species.

The greatest threat to the world's living creatures is the degradation and destruction of habitat, affecting nine out of 10 threatened species. Humans have transformed nearly half of the planet's ice-free land areas, with serious effects on the rest of nature. We have made agricultural fields out of prairies and forests. We have dammed rivers and drained wetlands. We have paved over soil to build cities and roads. . . .

Direct human exploitation of organisms, such as through hunting and harvesting, threatens more than one-third of the listed birds and mammals. Other threats to biodiversity include exotic species, often transported by humans, which can outcompete and displace native ones.

A survey of some 1,100 animal and plant species found that climate change could wipe out between 15–37% of them by 2050. Yet, the actual losses may be greater because of the complexity of natural systems. The extinction of key species could have cascading effects throughout the food chain. . . .

Time to Take Action

Consciously avoiding habitat destruction and mitigating the effects of land use alteration, reducing the direct exploitation of plants and wildlife, and slowing climate change can help us stop weakening the very life-support systems we depend on. While this may be the first time in history that a single species can precipitate a mass extinction event, it also is the only time that a single species can act to prevent it.

EVALUATING THE AUTHOR'S ARGUMENTS:

Janet Larsen uses many statistics to support her argument that species extinction is a serious problem. In your opinion, do statistics increase the effectiveness of her argument? Why or why not?

The Problem of Species Extinction Has Been Overstated

"The common claim that we're going to lose anywhere from 25 to 50 percent of all species in our lifetimes is simply not true."

Bjørn Lomborg

The following viewpoint is excerpted from an interview with Bjørn Lomborg, an associate professor of statistics at the University of Aarhus, Denmark. Although he admits that species extinction takes place because of human activity, he says the seriousness of this problem has been greatly exaggerated. The actual rate of extinction is far less than commonly claimed, says Lomborg. In his opinion, this exaggeration leads to environmental policies based on panic rather than common sense. Lomborg is the author of *The Skeptical Environmentalist: Measuring the Real State of the World.*

AS YOU READ, CONSIDER THE FOLLOWING QUESTIONS:

1. What are three common beliefs about the environment that Lomborg says are untrue?

2. In the author's opinion, what is the extinction rate estimated by most experts for the next fifty years?
3. Why must environmental problems be prioritized, according to Lomborg?

C risis *editor Brian Saint-Paul: In your book, you mention what you refer to as the "environmental litany." What is this?*
Bjørn Lomborg: It's the idea that everything is getting worse. That air pollution is getting worse, that there's not enough food, that we're despoiling the soil, that we're creating a world where things are going to hell and that—in the long term—we won't be able to sustain ourselves.

Misleading Portrayals
This is the common belief.

Definitely. And I document this with numerous quotes from a lot of different people. While this is how the issues are generally portrayed, it's wrong and it's not helping anyone understand them better. In reality, things are moving in the *right* direction. It's not getting worse and worse.

Although some animal species are threatened with extinction, many species, such as these zebra and wildebeest, are actually thriving.

Extinction Exaggerated

Give us a specific example of how your research contradicted one of the common environmental planks. Let's take biodiversity—the notion that species are becoming extinct left and right. Obviously, there are species that are disappearing, but is this the epidemic so often portrayed by activists?

We *are* causing some species extinction, simply because we have such a large presence in the world. So the discussion here is not whether or not it's happening—it is, and we need to face up to it. But we also need to get a sense of proportion in this. Where should we spend our limited resources? What kinds of priorities should we have?

But the common claim that we're going to lose anywhere from 25 to 50 percent of all species in our lifetimes is simply not true. It's not backed up by the data that we have. We've always lost species and we're losing more now than ever before. But most experts estimate around 0.7 percent over the next 50 years.

Look, if someone tells us we're going to lose 25 to 50 percent of our species in the next 50 years, then we'll go into a panic mode and will reach for any possible solution. After all, if that were true, it would be catastrophic.

Professor Bjørn Lomborg, right, has argued that the rate of species extinction has been grossly exaggerated.

Scientists say the Bengal tiger is threatened with extinction. The loss of species is a natural phenomenon that has always occurred.

A planet-changing phenomenon.

Right. And we'd need to go into an emergency mode. On the other hand, a loss of 0.7 percent is a problem—no question. But it's one problem among many problems. And there are other problems that may be more pressing. This is where prioritization comes into play.

The analogy I use is this: Imagine someone puts a gun to your head and tells you to do something. If that happened, you'd do it quickly, without thinking. You act out of a panic. This is what we must not do, or we're going to make mistakes.

There's no environmental gun to our head?

Right.

Prioritizing Problems

As a statistician, you can look at the big picture—you can crunch the numbers. But the environmental scientists are experts in their fields. They can pick up nuances that may be missed in the big picture. How is your macro-view different from what they're seeing? Surely, they're not lying about what they're reporting.

No, of course not. But everyone thinks that his own interest is the most important thing. That's a very common thing. Before I started doing this, I was working on game theory and computer simulation. Possibly a couple hundred people in the world really cared about what that was. And yet, I thought that was one of the really important areas of study. It's natural.

And so biologists feel uncomfortable when someone comes along and says, "Sure, we're losing species and that's a problem. But how does that problem compare to some of the others we've got? How big a problem is this really?" This question is outside their scope of discussion, and I understand that. But in a political society, we need to have those kinds of discussions. Because we're prioritizing between a lot of different problems. We only have so many resources to address these issues.

EVALUATING THE AUTHORS' ARGUMENTS:

In chapter 1, J. William Gibson and Janet Larsen maintain that there is an environmental crisis, while Alex A. Avery and Dennis T. Avery, and Bjørn Lomborg contend that environmental problems have been exaggerated. If you were to write an essay about whether an environmental crisis is approaching, what would be your opinion? What evidence would you use to support your case?

Chapter 2

What Threats Does the Environment Face?

Oil spills, such as this one off the coast of Wales, harm birds, fish, and other marine life.

Global Warming Will Reduce the World's Food Supply

Brian Halweil

"Farming may be . . . the industry that will struggle most to cope with more erratic weather."

Successful farming depends on stable weather conditions, explains Brian Halweil in the following viewpoint. Yet global warming is dramatically and unpredictably changing weather patterns around the world, he argues, making global food production more difficult. In addition, maintains Halweil, many studies show that the increased temperatures and carbon dioxide levels that result from global warming will decrease crop yields. He concludes that global warming will harm the world's food supply, particularly in developing nations. Halweil is a researcher at the Worldwatch Institute and the author of *Eat Here: Reclaiming Homegrown Pleasures in a Global Supermarket.*

Brian Halweil, "The Irony of Climate: Archaeologists Suspect That a Shift in the Planet's Climate Thousands of Years Ago Gave Birth to Agriculture. Now Climate Change Could Spell the End of Farming as We Know It," *World Watch,* vol. 18, March/April 2005, p. 18. Copyright © 2005 by the Worldwatch Institute, www.worldwatch.org. Reproduced by permission.

AS YOU READ, CONSIDER THE FOLLOWING QUESTIONS:

1. What do Hartwell Allen's experiments, as reported by Halweil, show about the effect of increased temperatures on plant growth?
2. According to Cynthia Rosenzweig, as cited by the author, why will global warming cause an increased incidence of crop pests?
3. In Halweil's opinion, how will global warming affect hunger in sub-Saharan Africa?

High in the Peruvian Andes, a new disease has invaded the potato fields in the town of Chacllabamba. Warmer and wetter weather associated with global climate change has allowed late blight—the same fungus that caused the Irish potato famine—to creep 4,000 meters up the mountainside for the first time since humans started growing potatoes here thousands of years ago. In 2003, Chacllabamba farmers saw their crop of native potatoes almost totally destroyed. Breeders are rushing to develop tubers resistant to the "new" disease that retain the taste, texture, and quality preferred by Andean populations. . . .

Changing Weather Patterns

Asian farmers, too, are facing their own climate-related problems. In the unirrigated rice paddies and wheat fields of Asia, the annual monsoon can make or break millions of lives. Yet the reliability of the monsoon is increasingly in doubt. For instance, El Niño events (the cyclical warming of surface waters in the eastern Pacific Ocean) often correspond with weaker monsoons, and El Niños will likely increase with global warming. During the El Niño–induced drought in 1997, Indonesian rice farmers pumped water from swamps close to their fields, but food losses were still high: 55 percent for dryland maize and 41 percent for wetland maize, 34 percent for wetland rice, and 19 percent for cassava. The 1997 drought was followed by a particularly wet winter that delayed planting for two months in many areas and triggered heavy locust and rat infestations. According to Bambang Irawan of the Indonesian Center for Agricultural Socio-Economic Research and Development, in Bogor, this succession of poor harvests forced many families to eat less rice and turn to the less nutritious

Some scientists maintain that warmer temperatures could lead to smaller crop yields, which could affect farmers like this potato harvester in Peru.

alternative of dried cassava. Some farmers sold off their jewelry and livestock, worked off the farm, or borrowed money to purchase rice, Irawan says. The prospects are for more of the same: "If we get a substantial global warming, there is no doubt in my mind that there will be serious changes to the monsoon," says David Rhind, a senior climate researcher with NASA [National Aeronautics and Space Administration]'s Goddard Institute for Space Studies.

Archaeologists believe that the shift to a warmer, wetter, and more stable climate at the end of the last ice age was key for humanity's successful foray into food production. Yet, from the American breadbasket to the North China Plain to the fields of southern Africa, farmers and climate scientists are finding that generations-old patterns of rainfall and temperature are shifting. Farming may be the human endeavor most dependent on a stable climate—and the industry that will struggle most to cope with more erratic weather, severe storms, and shifts in growing season lengths. While some optimists are predicting longer growing seasons and more abundant harvests as the climate warms, farmers are mostly reaping surprises.

Warmer Temperatures Damage Plants

For two decades, Hartwell Allen, a researcher with the University of Florida in Gainesville and the U.S. Department of Agriculture, has been growing rice, soybeans, and peanuts in plastic, greenhouse-like growth chambers that allow him to play God. He can control—"rather precisely"—the temperature, humidity, and levels of atmospheric carbon. "We grow the plants under a daily maximum/minimum cyclic temperature that would mimic the real world cycle," Allen says. His lab has tried regimes of 28 degrees C day/18 degrees C night, 32/22, 36/26, 40/30, and 44/34. "We ran one experiment to 48/38, and got very few surviving plants," he says. Allen found that while a doubling of carbon dioxide and a slightly increased temperature stimulate seeds to germinate and the plants to grow larger and lusher, the higher temperatures are deadly when the plant starts producing pollen. Every stage of the process—pollen transfer, the growth of the tube that links the pollen to the seed, the viability of the pollen itself—is highly sensitive. "It's all or nothing, if pollination isn't successful," Allen notes.

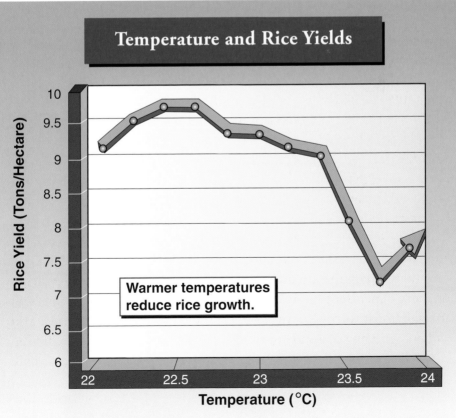

Temperature and Rice Yields

Rice Yield (Tons/Hectare)

Warmer temperatures reduce rice growth.

Temperature (°C)

Source: Shaobing Peng et al., *Proceedings of the National Academy of Sciences of the United States*, July 6, 2004.

At temperatures above 36 degrees C during pollination, peanut yields dropped about six percent per degree of temperature increase. Allen is particularly concerned about the implications for places like India and West Africa, where peanuts are a dietary staple and temperatures during the growing season are already well above 32 degrees C: "In these regions the crops are mostly rain-fed. If global warming also leads to drought in these areas, yields could be even lower."

The Threat of Unpredictability

As plant scientists refine their understanding of climate change and the subtle ways in which plants respond, they are beginning to think that the most serious threats to agriculture will not be the most dramatic: the lethal heatwave or severe drought or endless deluge. Instead, for plants that humans have bred to thrive in specific climatic conditions, it is those subtle shifts in temperatures and rainfall during key periods in the crops' lifecycles that will be most disruptive. Even today, crop losses associated with background climate variability are signif-

This watermelon crop in Kosovo was destroyed during a violent storm. Some scientists worry severe weather caused by climate change poses a threat to the world's food supply.

icantly higher than those caused by disasters such as hurricanes or flooding.

John Sheehy at the International Rice Research Institute in Manila has found that damage to the world's major grain crops begins when temperatures climb above 30 degrees C during flowering. At about 40 degrees C, yields are reduced to zero. "In rice, wheat, and maize, grain yields are likely to decline by 10 percent for every 1 degree C increase over 30 degrees. We are already at or close to this threshold," Sheehy says. . . . The world's major plants can cope with temperature shifts to some extent, but since the dawn of agriculture farmers have selected plants that thrive in stable conditions.

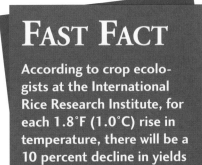

FAST FACT

According to crop ecologists at the International Rice Research Institute, for each 1.8°F (1.0°C) rise in temperature, there will be a 10 percent decline in yields of wheat, rice, and corn.

Climatologists consulting their computer climate models see anything but stability, however. As greenhouse gases trap more of the sun's heat in the Earth's atmosphere, there is also more energy in the climate system, which means more extreme swings—dry to wet, hot to cold. (This is the reason that there can still be severe winters on a warming planet, or that March 2004 was the third-warmest month on record after one of the coldest winters ever.) Among those projected impacts that climatologists have already observed in most regions: higher maximum temperatures and more hot days, higher minimum temperatures and fewer cold days, more variable and extreme rainfall events, and increased summer drying and associated risk of drought in continental interiors. All of these conditions will likely accelerate into the next century.

Harmful Changes Predicted

Cynthia Rosenzweig, a senior research scholar with the Goddard Institute for Space Studies at Columbia University, argues that although the climate models will always be improving, there are certain changes we can already predict with a level of confidence. First, most studies indicate "intensification of the hydrological cycle," which essentially means more droughts and floods, and more variable and extreme rainfall. Second, Rosenzweig says, "basically every study has shown that there will be increased incidence of crop pests." Longer growing seasons mean more generations of pests during the summer, while shorter and warmer winters mean that fewer adults, larvae, and eggs will die off.

Third, most climatologists agree that climate change will hit farmers in the developing world hardest. This is partly a result of geography. Farmers in the tropics already find themselves near the temperature limits for most major crops, so any warming is likely to push their crops over the top. "All increases in temperature, however small, will lead to decreases in production," says Robert Watson, chief scientist at the World Bank and former chairman of the Intergovernmental Panel on Climate Change. "Studies have consistently shown that agricultural regions in the developing world are more vulnerable, even before we consider the ability to cope," because of poverty, more limited irrigation technology, and lack of weather tracking systems. "Look at the coping strategies, and then it's a real double whammy," Rosenzweig says. In sub-Saharan Africa—ground zero of global hunger, where the number of starving people has doubled in the last 20 years—the current situation will undoubtedly be exacerbated by the climate crisis.

EVALUATING THE AUTHORS' ARGUMENTS:

The author of this viewpoint believes that global warming will be harmful to the world's food supply. How do you think Dennis J. Behreandt, the author of the next viewpoint, might respond to this argument?

Global Warming Will Increase the World's Food Supply

Dennis J. Behreandt

"With more CO_2 in the air . . . plants grow bigger and better in almost every conceivable way."

In the following viewpoint Dennis J. Behreandt argues that higher carbon dioxide (CO_2) levels caused by global warming will increase crop yields around the world. According to Behreandt, scientific theory and numerous experiments have shown that greater concentrations of carbon dioxide enhance plant growth and reproduction. He concludes that fears about the harmful impacts of global warming on plants are misguided. Behreandt is a contributing writer to the *New American,* a biweekly conservative newsmagazine.

AS YOU READ, CONSIDER THE FOLLOWING QUESTIONS:
1. What does plant growth depend on, as explained by Behreandt?
2. What, according to the author, did a 2002 study of ragweed pollen show about the effect of increases in carbon dioxide?
3. According to Behreandt, in addition to stimulating plant growth and reproduction, what else do elevated carbon dioxide levels allow plants to do?

I magine a world without carbon dioxide (CO_2). It would be a world without life. Plants of all kinds, from the greatest of the world's stately trees to the smallest single-celled algae, would disappear. Gone too would be the herbivorous creatures, including the elk and deer of the forest and the ox and horse of the pasture. Without the herbivores to prey upon, the great carnivores would disappear as well. Finally, without the plants and the animals, man too would disappear.

As every schoolchild knows, plants need CO_2, and the food chain, leading inexorably to man, depends upon plants. Fortunately, there is no shortage of CO_2 in the atmosphere and the Earth's plant life continues to thrive. In fact, as Danish environmentalist Bjørn Lomborg notes in his book, *The Skeptical Environmentalist,* the amount of forested land in the world has been stable and may have grown.

Now, imagine a world in which CO_2 is increasing. Indeed, this is now the case. But what will be the result? Will plant growth benefit? Will crop yields improve? Will the Earth actually become greener? Even a rudimentary knowledge of CO_2—one of the molecules blamed for "global warming"—would suggest that the answer to all of these questions must be yes. In fact, scientists know that an increase in the amount of CO_2 in the atmosphere would benefit plant life not only on the basis of our understanding of the science but on the basis of experimentation.

The Stuff of Life

The carbon dioxide molecule is composed of one carbon atom and two oxygen atoms. A gas, CO_2 serves as the principal repository from which carbon is drawn for the construction of organic compounds. These include simple sugars, like sucrose ($C_6H_{12}O_6$), as well as the more complex carbohydrates. These compounds, which form an essential link in the chemical chain reactions of life, are created by autotrophic organisms—plants—that gather carbon and energy from the environment, carbon from carbon dioxide, and energy from sunlight.

Carbon dioxide, a gas found in automobile emissions and other sources, is essential for plant growth.

The means by which plants do this is photosynthesis, a process requiring both light and carbon dioxide. Of the reactions involved, those that require CO_2 result in the construction of carbohydrates, including starches and sugars. This process begins with carbon fixation and is initiated when carbon dioxide in the air diffuses into the leaves of plants and into spaces between photosynthetic cells. There, enzymatic activity captures the carbon atoms that are then used by the plant to construct necessary carbohydrates. Plant growth depends on the efficient utilization of carbon dioxide.

Dr. Sherwood Idso currently serves as president of the Center for the Study of Carbon Dioxide and Global Change, a post he's held since 2001. Prior to that time, Dr. Idso served as a research physicist with the U.S. Department of Agriculture's Water Conservation Laboratory in Phoenix, Arizona. In experiments conducted with orange trees, Dr. Idso found that increases in carbon dioxide led to increased growth in orange crops.

Dr. Idso's experiments showing a correlation between increased levels of CO_2 and increased plant growth have been confirmed by results obtained by similar studies conducted by other scientists using other species. The Center for the Study of Carbon Dioxide and Global Change maintains a database, available online, tracking the startling results of many of these studies.

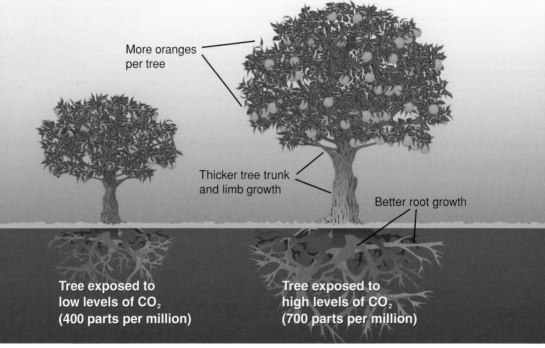

Global Warming Can Help Plants Grow

A study on orange trees found that they benefited from being exposed to higher levels of carbon dioxide (CO_2), a gas believed to contribute to global warming.

More oranges per tree

Thicker tree trunk and limb growth

Better root growth

Tree exposed to low levels of CO_2 (400 parts per million)

Tree exposed to high levels of CO_2 (700 parts per million)

Source: Arthur B. Robinson et al., Oregon Institute of Science and Medicine, 2001. www.oism.org.

A Greener Globe

In the studies tracked by the center, results were obtained with the equivalent of a 300 part per million (ppm) increase over current ambient CO_2 levels. According to the National Oceanic and Atmospheric Administration monitoring station at Hawaii's Mauna Loa observatory, current atmospheric carbon dioxide levels hover near 379 ppm. In the center's tracking of studies done on wheat, for instance, the majority of findings indicate that the addition of 300 ppm of CO_2 to the atmosphere leads to large increases in wheat biomass. . . .

This has major implications for the well-being of mankind. With increasing CO_2 levels, all sorts of crops, including wheat, can be expected to be more productive, increasing the food supply. This fact is never cited by those who, like Paul Ehrlich and other Malthusian population controllers,[1] agitate for governmental limits on the growth of human

1. In 1798 economist Thomas Malthus predicted that Earth's population would eventually outrun its food supply.

populations. This is perhaps because many of those advocating harsh population-control measures are also vocal global warming alarmists. Good news simply doesn't fit their political agenda. Nevertheless, it is clear that higher levels of CO_2 have the potential to benefit man.

It is not just plant growth that is encouraged by elevated levels of CO_2. The suggestive findings of one study indicate that plant reproduction may also benefit. In findings published in the journal *Annals of Allergy, Asthma and Immunology* in 2002, scientists Peter Wayne, Susannah Foster, John Connolly, Fakhri Bazzaz and Paul Epstein found that ragweed pollen production is increased substantially when high levels of CO_2 are present. . . .

The authors of the ragweed study note in their conclusions that the results they obtained are consistent with those of other, similar studies. . . . In fact, such conclusions have become widespread. Writing in the *Encyclopedia of Global Environmental Change*, Hendrik Poorter of Utrecht University in the Netherlands and Marta Pérez-Soba of Plant Research International noted, "Elevated carbon dioxide (CO_2) concentrations stimulate the rate of photosynthesis of most plant species. Consequently, it is expected that prolonged growth of plants at increased

Several studies support the idea that a carbon dioxide rich atmosphere might lead to a greener planet.

atmospheric CO_2 concentrations will enhance their biomass. This prediction is in agreement with most experimental results performed at optimal growth conditions."

The CO_2 Future

Not only do elevated concentrations of CO_2 stimulate plant growth and reproduction, they also allow plants to adapt to warmer temperatures. Poorter and Pérez-Soba point out that "Elevated atmospheric carbon dioxide (CO_2) concentrations generally have two direct and momentary physiological effects on plants. First, they increase the rate of photosynthesis of the leaves, because of higher CO_2 concentrations at the sites where enzymes fix CO_2. Second, they cause stomata[2] to partly close, thereby reducing the water loss due to transpiration." This second effect allows plants to adapt to and flourish in drier conditions featuring higher ambient temperatures.

Environmental extremists and their allies in government and the media tend to portray the future as one of impending disaster brought on by CO_2-induced global warming. Reality, though, is far different from these gloomy predictions. As Drs. Craig and Keith Idso of the Center for the Study of Carbon Dioxide and Global Change write, "With more CO_2 in the air, literally thousands of experiments have *proven*, beyond any doubt, that plants grow bigger and better in almost every conceivable way, and they do it more *efficiently*, with respect to the availability of important natural resources, and more *effectively*, in the face of various environmental constraints." (Emphasis in original.) Instead of environmental disaster, in a world with a CO_2-enriched atmosphere, the future will be green with abundance.

2. tiny pores on the underside of a plant leaf

EVALUATING THE AUTHOR'S ARGUMENTS:

What evidence does the author use to support his argument that global warming will increase the world's food supply? Do you find this evidence convincing? Explain.

America's Marine Resources Are Threatened

Kate Wing

"Years of treating the ocean as the last frontier— inexhaustible and open 24 hours a day— have taken their toll."

America's oceans are rich in natural resources, but these resources are exhaustible, states Kate Wing in the following viewpoint. In her opinion, the United States has largely ignored this fact, and the oceans are suffering from overuse. She calls for the creation of marine reserves to help preserve healthy ocean ecosystems before they are destroyed. Wing served on the staff of the U.S. Senate Subcommittee for Oceans and Fisheries, and she has worked on management of many of California's fisheries.

AS YOU READ, CONSIDER THE FOLLOWING QUESTIONS:

1. According to Wing, how does America's treatment of its land differ from that of its oceans?
2. Name five ways in which human activity impacts the ocean, according to the author.
3. Wing describes marine reserves as "precautionary." What does the word *precautionary* mean in this context?

W̲e̲ live in an ocean country. The United States controls the waters stretching out to 200 nautical miles from the shore, an area of sea as large as the total land in all fifty states. Inside the waters of this ocean country live some of the most extraordinary communities of plants and animals on earth. Because the United States stretches across latitudes from the arctic to the tropics, our oceans contain a greater amount of diversity than almost any other nation. Millions of Americans head to the sea each year to experience this marine biodiversity: in Alaskan bays filled with sea lions and salmon; along sandy beaches in the Gulf of Mexico; on delicate coral reefs around the Hawaiian Islands; and in the rocky tidepools of New England and Washington. There is tremendous wealth in our sea, and we draw on its resources every day. How can we make sure that these rich ocean ecosystems survive for future generations?

Taking Too Much

All too often the only news about the ocean is bad news. Fisheries are crashing as more boats chase increasingly fewer fish. Oil spills and

A fishing crew in Alaskan waters sorts through a net of salmon. Overfishing poses a threat to fish populations around the world.

'I like to recreate their natural environment'

Linden. © by Punch. Reproduced by permission of Rothco Cartoons, Inc.

sewage pollute the beaches. Heavy trawl fishing gear scrapes the ocean floor bare, disturbing underwater wildlife. Corals are shattered by boat anchors or die from disease and pollution. Last year [2000] scientists working with the American Fisheries Society identified 82 marine fishes at risk of becoming extinct in the near future. Years of treating the ocean as the last frontier—inexhaustible and open 24 hours a day—have taken their toll.

We rely on poor and incomplete information about the ocean's condition and we have erred on the side of taking more, not less. When the National Marine Fisheries Service published its most recent report on the status of fish populations, the most shocking figure was not the 106 populations considered to be overfished. It was the fact that over two-thirds of species that are actively fished are considered "unknown," meaning that the service has no idea of the condition of those stocks. With such a poor understanding of the ocean, marine plants and animals can disappear completely unnoticed.

Marine Reserves

On land, we safeguard our natural heritage with a system of protected areas. There are national and state parks, monuments, wilderness areas, and wildlife refuges, some over a hundred years old. We restrict what activities can occur in these places to protect our wildlife, and we make provisions so that the public can enjoy them. Below the high tide line, we are only beginning to protect wilderness. Currently [in 2001], less than one-hundredth of 1 percent of U.S. waters is fully protected, i.e., closed to all extractive uses, such as oil drilling, mining, or fishing. Yet these few ocean wilderness areas, or marine reserves, produce a tremendous amount of good news. Inside marine reserves there are more fish, larger fish, and healthier habitat than outside, where the ocean is everyone's property and no one's responsibility. Marine reserves around the world have demonstrated their ability to preserve healthy ecosystems, protect biodiversity, and rebuild depleted fish populations. . . .

FAST FACT

According to the Pew Oceans Commission, at least a third of U.S. fish stocks are currently being overfished.

Constantly Disturbing the Ocean

The oceans form the largest highway in the world, carrying thousands of cargo ships each day. Sailboats race across them, and kayakers meander along their coastlines. We mine them for gravel and sand, and we dump our waste into them. We fish in them, both for food and just for the thrill of a catch. The oceans hold dive sites, oil wells, fiber-optic cables, surfing grounds, and holy places. More than half the U.S. population lives within 50 miles of the coastline, increasing the development that spills pollution into the sea. Federal and state governments juggle all these uses simultaneously, trying to keep everyone from colliding. When they focus on avoiding conflicts among different uses, they can easily overlook the larger impact of allowing so much activity in any one place. Marine reserves are based on the simple idea of leaving parts of the sea undisturbed.

The cumulative impacts of constantly disturbing the ocean can have devastating effects in the long term. Fish diminish in size and number or disappear altogether. Fishing gear can destroy sea grasses, corals, and other habitats. Taking large numbers of a species not only impacts the population of that species, but also the populations of its prey and its predators. Fishermen often target groups of fish with similar behavior or habitat preferences—such as all fish resting on an area of the sea floor, or all fish feeding in a certain area. This can include many different species that fill similar ecological roles. When this happens, overfishing can completely eliminate a level of the food chain and shift the dynamics of the entire system. Where once there were schools of large predatory fish, now there may only be tiny fish feeding on plankton. . . .

Even when fishing is drastically reduced or stopped altogether, it may take fifty to one hundred years for a population of fish to recover to even half of its initial size. Mandatory plans to rebuild fish populations are a new part of U.S. law, but so far very few programs have

A surfer in San Diego rides a wave as a barge dumps sand dredged from a nearby beach. Increasing use and traffic can take a heavy toll on the ocean.

been successful. Fishing boats now have the skill and technology to catch in a few seasons what can take decades to replace. Fishing down the food chain is unsustainable, not only for fishermen but also for the ocean wildlife like seals and otters which subsist on fish. Combine heavy fishing pressure with other human activities, like pollution and dredging, and larger environmental changes, like shifting ocean temperature regimes, and you have a recipe for disaster.

Precautionary Action

Marine reserves offer insurance for marine ecosystems—insurance against natural changes and errors in judgment and management. Effective management policies, including sound fisheries management and pollution control, are essential for healthy oceans. Reserves cannot work without the support of these other policies. But too often agencies act after a problem is discovered. Marine reserves are precautionary; they are an action we can take now, before problems arise, rather than waiting until it is too late.

EVALUATING THE AUTHORS' ARGUMENTS:

Kate Wing believes that as a result of overuse, America's oceans are in crisis. Conrad Lautenbacher, the author of the next viewpoint, disagrees. He believes that the state of America's marine resources has greatly improved. What evidence does each author use to support her or his argument? In your opinion, whose argument is more persuasive? Why?

America's Marine Resources Are Healthy

Conrad Lautenbacher

"[Ocean management has resulted in the] successful rebuilding and sustainable harvesting of our nation's fisheries."

In the following viewpoint Conrad Lautenbacher maintains that the health of America's oceans has greatly improved and will continue to do so in the future. He believes America is managing its marine resources in an effective and sustainable manner. According to Lautenbacher, many fish stocks have rebounded, marine habitats have been restored, and better data collection and ocean research is taking place. Lautenbacher is administrator of the National Oceanic and Atmospheric Administration, a scientific agency of the U.S. Department of Commerce that focuses on the conditions of the oceans and the atmosphere.

AS YOU READ, CONSIDER THE FOLLOWING QUESTIONS:
1. How many rebuilding programs have been developed and implemented for stocks that are overfished, according to the author?
2. According to Lautenbacher, what is the economic impact of the recreational fishing industry in the United States?
3. Why did NOAA launch four survey vessels in 2003, as explained by the author?

Conrad Lautenbacher, speech before a conference on fisheries management in the United States, Washington, DC, November 13–15, 2003.

Environmental legislation such as the Magnuson-Stevens Act of 1996 has helped repopulate many once-threatened fish populations, benefiting fishers like this one.

It's been over 25 years since Congress passed the Magnuson-Stevens Fishery Conservation and Management Act, one of several environmental laws that were passed in the 1970s. During that time the public focused its attention on the health and welfare of our nation's oceans. This unprecedented interest ushered in a suite of marine conservation laws that reshaped the way Americans viewed marine resources, our stewardship responsibilities, and the need to invest in marine science and management of ocean resources to redress excesses of the past and ensure a sustainable future. Developed in 1976, the Magnuson-Stevens Act provides for federal management of fisheries in the 200-mile U.S. Exclusive Economic Zone.[1] . . .

Managing America's Marine Resources

The fisheries management process established by the Magnuson-Stevens Act is a dynamic and successful management regime that has evolved to meet new challenges. . . .

1. Under International Maritime Law, countries have special rights over the exploration and use of marine resources within a certain distance from their coast. America's Exclusive Economic Zone extends 200 miles.

Evaluating the effectiveness of the nation's fisheries management process must be viewed as an evolutionary process that continues today. After more than 25 years, the collaborative stewardship between NOAA [National Oceanic and Atmospheric Administration] Fisheries, the regional councils, and our constituents has produced a world-class body of science and management strategies that are leading the way toward ecosystem management, international stewardship, and most importantly, the successful rebuilding and sustainable harvesting of our nation's fisheries.

Responding to the increasing challenges facing fisheries management, Congress overhauled the Magnuson-Stevens Act in 1996, through a reauthorization known as the Sustainable Fisheries Act or SFA. . . .

Recent Achievements

The SFA provided NOAA Fisheries with a number of necessary tools to meet the challenges of the new millennium as world-class leaders in fishery stewardship. The agency has placed a stronger emphasis on reducing bycatch,[2] protecting marine habitats, halting overfishing, and rebuilding fish stocks to sustainable levels. We already have seen many fish stocks rebound as a direct result of the changes to the Magnuson-Stevens Act. However, the true magnitude of our achievements has yet to be realized, as these sweeping changes to the Act have been in place for a relatively short period of time. It will likely take many years before the results can be fully realized. In the meantime, NOAA Fisheries has made a number of important strides for which I would like to commend them.

> **FAST FACT**
>
> New fishing technology is helping to end harmful fishing practices. For example, by modifying the shape of their hooks and switching to a different type of bait, fishers in the western North Atlantic were able to reduce accidental turtle catch by 92 percent, while increasing the catch of their target species.

Status of the Stocks

Key to achieving sustainable fisheries is the need to rebuild depleted

2. Bycatch is fish or shellfish caught accidentally while harvesting other species. For example, dolphins that get accidentally caught in tuna nets are bycatch.

stocks. Though fish stocks will take many years to recover from over-fishing practices of the past, the councils and NOAA Fisheries are well on the way toward meeting this challenge. [Since 1998] we have reduced the number of stocks from both the overfished and overfishing categories, for a net gain of 13 stocks taken off the overfished list (20 removed, 7 added) and 14 off the overfishing list (26 removed, 12 added). In addition, 70 rebuilding programs have been developed and implemented for stocks that are overfished.

Rebuilding a depleted stock to a point where it can be fished sustainably is the desired outcome best for the environment and the economy. NOAA Fisheries and the Regional Fisheries Management Councils strongly believe we should do what we can to preserve fishing as an important part of local economies and the overall national economy. Fishing communities are an important part of the fabric of the American way of life.

In the few short years since implementing the SFA, we already have begun to witness the benefits of stewardship and sustainable harvests. For example, in 2002, commercial fishermen brought 908.1 million pounds of fish and shellfish to the port of Dutch Harbor–Unalaska,

The ultimate goal of many agencies that work to protect both the environment and the economy is to achieve sustainable fish populations.

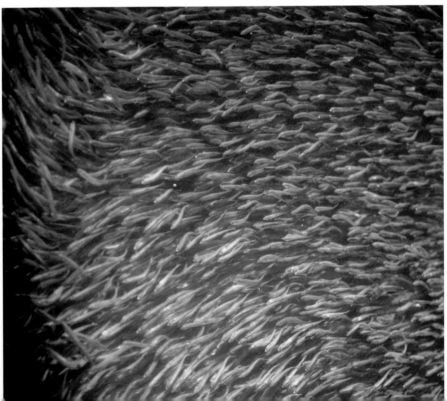

A fish-farm worker in Canada nets salmon from a pen. Once listed as an endangered species, salmon stocks have increased dramatically in recent years in some parts of the Pacific Ocean.

Alaska—an increase of 73.6 million pounds over 2001 landings—surpassing the 32-year volume record of 848.2 million pounds held by the port in Los Angeles, California. As the world's fifth largest fishing nation, our total commercial landings in 2002 totaled 9.4 billion pounds, worth $3.1 billion. . . .

Additionally, the recreational fishing industry in the United States makes an enormous contribution to the U.S. economy. Over 17 million Americans participated in recreational fishing in 2002, making over 65 million fishing trips and supporting almost 350,000 jobs with an economic impact of more than $30 billion. Healthy fish stocks are critical to maintaining this economic base.

Habitat Restoration

Part of rebuilding stocks is not only to lessen fishing pressures on certain species, but to provide more habitat for fish for every stage in their lifespan. I am thrilled to be able to say that ESA [Endangered Species Act]-listed Pacific salmon stocks are more abundant, in some cases up to 800% over recent lows, due in part to investment in habitat restoration and conservation partnerships. In 2003, NOAA also initiated 200 new grass-roots fishery restoration projects that will restore 3000 acres of habitat through dedicated funding to national and regional partners. The science of restoration is still young, but something that deserves more of our resources.

Better Data Collection and Research

Another critical area of study for NOAA Fisheries is to continue improving the quality and quantity of fisheries research data in order to better manage our living marine resources. I am pleased to be able to say that NOAA is doing something about that in a big way. On October 17 [2003], we launched the first of four planned NOAA fisheries survey vessels to either augment or replace aging ships in the NOAA fleet. . . . These ships will provide higher quality data to fisheries managers about targeted fish populations and the environment that sustains them. . . .

Sustainable Management

The fisheries management process has undergone dramatic change since the 1970s, when eliminating foreign fishing and developing domestic fisheries were the primary objectives. Today, the regional management framework has become a leading forum for advancing science-based management of living marine resources. Together, the Regional Fishery Management Councils and NOAA Fisheries continue managing our ocean resources for the maximum benefit to the nation, ensuring long-term recreational fishing opportunities for the American public, supporting coastal communities and fishing families, and maintaining a sustainable seafood supply.

EVALUATING THE AUTHOR'S ARGUMENTS:

Lautenbacher works for the National Oceanic and Atmospheric Administration, a government agency that conducts research and gathers data about the oceans, atmosphere, space, and sun. Does knowing this information influence your opinion of his argument? If so, in what way?

Air Pollution Is a Threat to Health in America

U.S. Public Interest Research Group

"Air pollution continues to pose a grave health threat to Americans."

In the following viewpoint the U.S. Public Interest Research Group (U.S. PIRG) maintains that a large number of Americans are forced to breathe unhealthy air. Levels of both ozone and fine particle pollution are high in many parts of the country, states U.S. PIRG. According to the group, many studies have shown that these pollutants cause a wide range of health problems. Air pollution will continue to harm Americans, argues U.S. PIRG, until the government takes action to reduce it. U.S. PIRG is an advocacy group that fights threats to public well-being through investigative research, media exposés, grassroots organizing, and litigation.

AS YOU READ, CONSIDER THE FOLLOWING QUESTIONS:
1. What does ozone do to the body, according to U.S. PIRG?
2. According to the American Lung Association, as cited by the author, how many Americans live in places with unhealthy levels of ozone?
3. According to U.S. PIRG, why do lower levels of ozone not necessarily mean that air pollution has been successfully reduced?

While air quality has improved in the last three decades, half of all Americans live in counties where air pollution exceeds national health standards. Most of these places suffer from high levels of ozone and/or particle pollution. Ozone is the country's most pervasive air pollutant; particle pollution is the nation's deadliest air pollutant. Coal-fired power plants and motor vehicles are the largest sources of these pollutants. This report, which is based on a comprehensive survey of environmental agencies from all 50 states and the District of Columbia, examines levels of ozone and fine particle pollution in cities and towns across the country in 2003 and finds that air pollution continues to pose a grave health threat to Americans. . . .

The Danger of Ozone Exposure

Exposure to even very low levels of ozone contributes to a wide range of adverse health effects. Ozone is a powerful oxidant that burns our lungs and airways, causing them to become inflamed, reddened, and swollen. According to the American Lung Association, nearly half (47 percent) of all Americans live in places with unhealthy levels of ozone. Children, senior citizens, and people with respiratory disease are particularly vulnerable to the health effects of ozone.

Following a lengthy scientific review process, in 1997 EPA [the Environmental Protection Agency] tightened the national ambient air quality standard for ozone. Based on extensive evidence of the risks posed by ozone at lower concentrations and over longer periods of exposure, EPA set the new standard at 0.08 parts per million (ppm) averaged over an eight-hour period. The new "8-hour standard" is more protective than the 1979 "1-hour standard" of 0.12 ppm averaged over one hour.

When EPA tightened the standard, the agency concluded that, when inhaled even at very low levels, ozone can cause chest pain and cough, aggravate asthma, reduce lung function, increase emergency room visits and hospital admissions for respiratory problems, and lead to irreversible lung damage.

Since 1997, more than 1,700 additional studies on the health and environmental effects of ozone have been published in peer-reviewed journals. These studies point to additional, even more serious health effects associated with exposure to ozone. . . .

While high ozone concentrations pose pervasive health risks and may be even more serious than previously believed, research demonstrates that declines in ozone levels can reduce these effects. For instance, during the 1996 Summer Olympics, officials closed downtown Atlanta to traffic and increased public transit, which reduced ozone levels and significantly lowered rates of acute care visits and hospitalizations for asthma among children.

Fine Particle Pollution

Fine particles are so small that they can bypass the body's natural defenses and penetrate some of the most fragile parts of the lung, causing

Ozone, America's most common air pollutant, can cause chest pain, coughing, and reduced lung function.

serious respiratory and cardiovascular problems. The American Heart Association recently concluded, "Although exposure to ambient air pollution poses smaller relative risks for incident cardiovascular disease than obesity or tobacco smoking, because it is ubiquitous, the absolute number of people affected is enormous, and exposure occurs over an entire lifetime." According to the American Lung Association, one quarter of Americans live in areas with unhealthy levels of fine particle pollution. A 2004 study by Abt Associates found that fine particles from U.S. power plants alone cause 554,000 asthma attacks, 38,200 non-fatal heart attacks, and 23,600 premature deaths, including 2,800 from lung cancer, every year. Senior citizens, people with heart and lung diseases, and children are most vulnerable to particle pollution.

After an extensive scientific review process, in 1997 EPA established the first national ambient air quality standards for fine particles. EPA concluded that exposure to fine particles is associated with premature death, increased hospital admissions and emergency room visits, increased respiratory symptoms and disease, and decreased lung function. Both short-term (few hours or days) and chronic exposure to particle pollution are associated with illness and death. . . .

FAST FACT

Smoggiest Metropolitan Areas

1. Los Angeles, CA
2. Bakersfield, CA
3. Fresno, CA
4. Visalia, CA
5. Houston, TX
6. Atlanta, GA
7. Merced, CA
8. Knoxville, TN
9. Charlotte, NC
10. Sacramento, CA

As with ozone, evidence suggests that reducing particle pollution would greatly and rapidly improve public health. For instance, air quality in Dublin, Ireland deteriorated in the 1980s after a switch from oil to coal for domestic heating. In 1990, the Irish Government banned the marketing, sale, and distribution of coal within Dublin. Respiratory and cardiovascular death rates fell markedly following the ban, with researchers concluding that "control of particulate air pollution in Dublin led to an immediate reduction in cardiovascular and respiratory deaths." . . .

The Environmental Protection Agency has identified hundreds of American cities, including Los Angeles (pictured), that have an unusually high concentration of ozone in the air.

EPA establishes health-based air quality standards for the six criteria pollutants, including ozone and fine particles, and identifies areas that fail to meet the standards as "nonattainment" areas. Nonattainment areas must take certain steps to clean up their air and meet the standards, as determined by Congress and EPA.

Violation of Ozone Standards

In April 2004, EPA determined that 474 counties violate or contribute to violations of the 8-hour health-based ozone standard. These counties—from large metropolitan areas like Los Angeles and Washington, D.C., to suburban and even rural areas like Lake County, Illinois, whose 470 square miles stretch from the Chicago suburbs to Wisconsin, and Christian County, a largely agricultural area in southwest Kentucky—are home to nearly 160 million people. These nonattainment areas must submit plans to EPA in April 2007 as to how they will meet the ozone standard by 2007–2021, depending on the severity of their ozone pollution.

In addition, 237 counties—home to 111 million Americans—continue to violate the 1-hour ozone standard. . . .

Action Needed

Until policymakers require tough cleanup standards for power plant smokestacks, Americans will continue to suffer serious health problems from ozone and fine particle pollution. Power plant pollution causes tens of thousands of premature deaths and many more asthma attacks, respiratory, and cardiovascular illnesses each year as well as a host of other health and environmental problems.

EVALUATING THE AUTHORS' ARGUMENTS:

In the viewpoint you just read, U.S. PIRG argues that air pollution is a serious health threat in the United States. In the next viewpoint, Joel Schwartz contends that the extent of America's air pollution has been exaggerated. After reading both viewpoints, what is your opinion? Cite from the text to support your position.

The Extent of America's Air Pollution Has Been Exaggerated

Joel Schwartz

"Never have smog levels been anywhere near this low."

Warnings about dangerous levels of air pollution in the United States have been greatly exaggerated, argues Joel Schwartz in the following viewpoint. According to Schwartz, activist groups and the media have manipulated the facts in order to overstate the extent of pollution. In reality, he says, air pollution levels have actually improved dramatically in the past few years. He predicts they will continue to improve. Schwartz is a senior fellow with Reason Public Policy Institute, a public-policy think tank. He is the author of the report "Finding Better Ways to Achieve Clean Air."

AS YOU READ, CONSIDER THE FOLLOWING QUESTIONS:

1. What is the single largest factor affecting year-to-year variations in smog levels, according to Schwartz?

2. In the author's opinion, why do activists avoid mentioning reductions in pollution levels?
3. According to Schwartz, what do data from around the country show about the relationship between hospitalizations and levels of ozone?

I n 2004, the United States reported the lowest ozone smog levels since states began measuring them in the 1970s. Based on preliminary data from around the country, the number of days exceeding the EPA's [Environmental Protection Agency]'s tough new eight-hour ozone standard declined to an average of about 50 percent below 2003, which was itself a record low year.

A combination of continuing emission reductions and favorable weather explains the improvements. Weather is the single largest factor affecting year-to-year variations in smog levels. All else equal, cool, wet, and windy years will have less ozone than warm, dry, and calm ones.

But weather is only part of the story. During the past 30 years, most of the country has had several years that were cooler and/or wetter than 2004, but never have smog levels been anywhere near this low. . . .

Biased Press Misleading Public

You wouldn't know this from reading activists' reports on air quality, which continue to tell a deceitfully gloomy story. *Dangerous Days of Summer* from Environmental Defense (ED) and *Danger in the Air* from the Public Interest Research Group (PIRG) are the two latest entries. Neither report mentions that 2003 and 2004 were the best years in history for ozone.

PIRG does mention that 2003 and 2004 were better than 2002, but attributes it all to weather.

Nevertheless, as you might expect, activists are always ready with a press release in years when measured air pollution rises. When ozone levels spiked upward during the hot, dry summer of 2002, a Clean Air Trust press release proclaimed "New Survey Finds Massive Smog Problem in 2002." But no activist press releases highlighted the spectacular decline in ozone levels the next year, nor the record-low ozone levels of the past two years.

Other potential but unmentioned contributors to the recent ozone improvements are a 60 percent reduction in coal-fired power plant NOx [nitrogen dioxide] emissions during the May–September "ozone season," . . . and an ongoing reduction of about 8 percent per year in total automobile emissions due to fleet turnover to cleaner vehicles.

Activists avoid mentioning these reductions because they undermine claims that urban "sprawl" increases air pollution and that power-plant emissions are increasing.

Full Range of Deceptions

ED's *Dangerous Days* commits the full range of deceptions pioneered by the American Lung Association (ALA) in its annual *State of the Air* series, such as: inflating pollution levels, exaggerating the harm from current air pollution levels and the number of people living in areas that exceed EPA standards, downplaying positive trends, and creating the impression that there will be little or no future improvement without stringent new regulations.

Some experts argue that cool, wet weather has helped curb air pollution in countries across the world.

For example, *Dangerous Days* claims the New York metro area exceeded the eight-hour ozone standard on 22 percent of summer days during 2001–2003. But the average site in the New York area exceeded the eight-hour standard on 10 percent of summer days—less than half of ED's claim. . . .

Exaggerating the Affected Population

Dangerous Days also exaggerates the number of people who live in areas that violate EPA's air standards. According to the report, "Nearly 160 million Americans live in areas where ozone smog levels exceed national standards. . . . Some 99 million Americans live in areas that exceed annual fine particle standards."

Both of these numbers are based on the populations of entire counties designated as "non-attainment" areas by EPA. But that has little to do with actual pollution levels where people live, because EPA designates whole regions as non-attainment areas even if only a single monitoring location violates a federal standard.

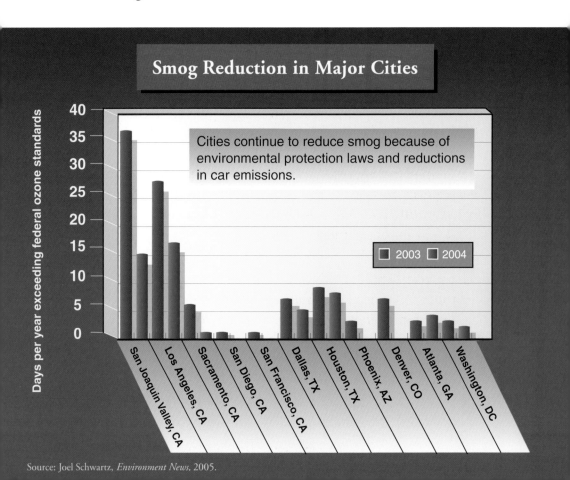

Smog Reduction in Major Cities

Cities continue to reduce smog because of environmental protection laws and reductions in car emissions.

Days per year exceeding federal ozone standards

☐ 2003 ☐ 2004

San Joaquin Valley, CA; Los Angeles, CA; Sacramento, CA; San Diego, CA; San Francisco, CA; Dallas, TX; Houston, TX; Phoenix, AZ; Denver, CO; Atlanta, GA; Washington, DC

Source: Joel Schwartz, *Environment News*, 2005.

That makes sense for air quality planning, but not for determining human exposure to air pollution. Thus, 94 to 99 percent of people in Chicago, Los Angeles, Phoenix, and San Diego live in areas that meet all EPA ozone standards, but EPA counts everyone in those areas as breathing dirty air. Environmental Defense used this counting method to mislead and cry wolf. . . .

FAST FACT

According to the Foundation for Clean Air Progress, since 1970 Americans have cut releases of air pollutants by more than 50 million tons.

Overstated Asthma Danger

Dangerous Days also implies air pollution is responsible for rising asthma rates: "Asthma has increasingly gained attention as a nationwide epidemic and a symbol of the manifold health impacts of air pollution. It is the nation's fastest growing chronic disease. . . ." Yet air pollution can't be a cause of rising asthma, because air pollution of all kinds has been falling nationwide at the same time asthma has been rising.

Air pollution can aggravate pre-existing respiratory disease, but its impact is nothing close to what groups such as ED claim. For example, when the [President Bill] Clinton-era EPA developed the eight-hour ozone standard, it predicted that going from full national attainment of the one-hour standard to full national attainment of the eight-hour standard would reduce hospital admissions for asthma by a mere 0.6 percent, despite the eight-hour standard's much greater stringency.

Data from around the United States show asthma hospitalizations are lowest in July and August—when levels of ozone and, in many areas PM [particulate matter] are highest.

Cooking the Books

Air pollution has gained the "national attention" referred to by ED not because of its overall importance as a cause of disease and disability, but because of its rhetorical power to generate eye-catching headlines, donations, and research funding.

I've often criticized the media for their mostly gloomy and misleading accounts of air quality issues. For example, despite the substantial

Some studies have found that despite a decrease in air pollution, asthma rates are on the rise.

decline in ozone exceedances since the 1970s, in an April 29, 2004, story on the American Lung Association's *State of the Air 2004* report, the *Washington Post* asserted, "Ozone pollution has declined *slightly* over the past 30 years" (emphasis added).

In 2004, however, many reporters around the country noticed the unusually low pollution levels reported by the EPA and let the public know about it. Even here, however, most stories gave the impression that mild weather was the sole cause, and they failed to discuss the long-term decline in smog-forming emissions or to compare smog levels in 2004 with much higher smog levels in previous years that had favorable weather.

Will air pollution remain just as low . . . ? That depends largely on the weather. But emissions will continue to decline, the long-term trend will continue downward . . . and environmental activists are sure to tell us the sky is falling.

EVALUATING THE AUTHORS' ARGUMENTS:

Three of the authors in chapter 2 argue that the environment is threatened, while the other three contend that this is not the case. If you were to write an essay on the state of the environment, what would be your opinion? What evidence would you use to support your case?

Chapter 3

What Should America's Environmental Policies Be?

Environmentalists protest a logging operation in Alaska. How best to protect the environment is a subject of ongoing controversy.

The Endangered Species Act Is Effective

Jamie Rappaport Clark

"The Endangered Species Act is one of our nation's most critical and essential environmental laws."

The Endangered Species Act (ESA) is vital to the protection of endangered species in the United States, maintains Jamie Rappaport Clark in the following viewpoint. Since its creation, the ESA has rescued hundreds of species from extinction, she argues, and preserved habitat critical to the survival of these species. In her opinion, the act must be preserved and strengthened. Clark is executive vice president of Defenders of Wildlife, an organization dedicated to protecting all native wild animals and plants.

AS YOU READ, CONSIDER THE FOLLOWING QUESTIONS:

1. According to Rappaport, extinction is now proceeding how much faster than the planet's historic rate?
2. What is the success rate of the Endangered Species Act, as argued by the author?
3. What does the word *prescient* mean in the context of this viewpoint?

Jamie Rappaport Clark, testimony before the U.S. Senate Subcommittee on Fisheries, Wildlife, and Water, Committee on the Environment and Public Works, Washington, DC, May 19, 2005.

For more than 30 years, the Endangered Species Act has sounded the alarm whenever wildlife faces extinction. Today, we have wolves in Yellowstone, manatees in Florida, and sea otters in California, largely because of the Act. We can still see bald eagles in the lower 48 states and other magnificent creatures like the peregrine falcon, the American alligator, and California condors, largely because of the Act.

Indeed, there can be no denying that, with the Endangered Species Act's help, hundreds of species have been rescued from the catastrophic permanence of extinction. Many have seen their populations stabilized; some have actually seen their populations grow. Some have even benefited from comprehensive recovery and habitat conservation efforts to the point where they no longer need the protections of the Act.

The Importance of the Act

In so many ways, Congress was prescient in the original construction of the Endangered Species Act. First, it crafted an Act that spoke specifically to the value—tangible and intangible—of conserving species for future generations, a key point sometimes lost in today's discussions.

Second, it addressed a problem that, at the time, was only just beginning to be understood: our looming extinction crisis. Currently there is little doubt left in the minds of professional biologists that Earth is faced with a mounting loss of species that threatens to rival the great mass extinctions of the geological record. Human activities have brought the Earth to the brink of this crisis. Many biologists today say that coming decades will see the loss of large numbers of species. These extinctions will alter not only biological diversity but also the evolutionary processes by which diversity is generated and maintained. Extinction is now proceeding one thousand times faster than the planet's historic rate.

FAST FACT

In the United States, 389 species of animals and 599 species of plants are currently listed as threatened or endangered.

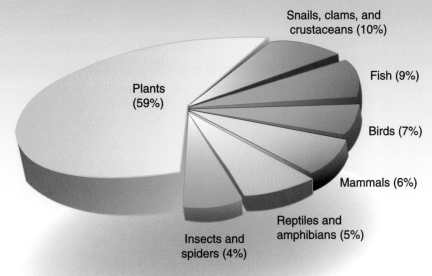

Species Listed as Endangered or Threatened in the United States

Snails, clams, and crustaceans (10%)

Fish (9%)

Plants (59%)

Birds (7%)

Mammals (6%)

Reptiles and amphibians (5%)

Insects and spiders (4%)

Source: U.S. Fish and Wildlife Service, 2003.

Lastly, in passing the Act, Congress recognized another key fact that subsequent scientific understanding has only confirmed: the best way to protect species is to conserve their habitat. Today, loss of habitat is widely considered by scientists to be the primary cause of species endangerment and extinction.

An Astonishing Success Rate

Reduced to its core, the Act simply says the federal government must identify species threatened with extinction, identify habitat they need to survive, and help protect both accordingly. And it has worked. Of the more than 1800 species currently protected by the Act, only 9 have been declared extinct. That's an astonishing more than 99% success rate. . . .

Unfortunately, opponents of the Act ignore these facts and call it a failure. They say we should dismantle the Act because it does not move enough species off the list to full recovery. They ignore the fact that the Act is our nation's best tool to prevent extinction and they ignore the hundreds of species still around today because of the Act's protections. And they ignore the simple truth that unless we prevent extinction first, there can never be any hope of recovery. . . .

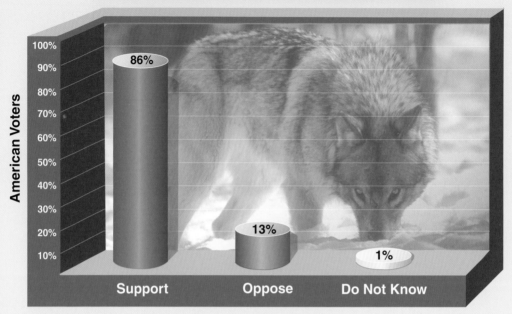

Position on the Endangered Species Act

American Voters

- 86% — Support
- 13% — Oppose
- 1% — Do Not Know

Source: Endangered Species Coalition, April 2004. www.stopextinction.org.

Making the Act Work Better

Although the Act is fundamentally sound, like any law, it can be improved. The more difficult question is whether the political process can accomplish that without succumbing to "false reforms" that actually weaken and undermine the law.

How can the Act be improved? Start by improving the protection and conservation of habitat. That means both more effective regulatory protection and more and better incentives to encourage voluntary habitat management and restoration, with species recovery as the overarching, governing standard. Incentives are especially important for private landowners, many of whom have demonstrated a keen eagerness to be true partners in species conservation. Let's also take the common sense step of linking the protection and conservation of habitat to the development and implementation of recovery plans. . . .

We need to make sure the federal government does its job too. We forget that it is not just the expert wildlife agencies that have a role in protecting and recovering listed species. All departments and agencies of the federal government have an affirmative obligation, expressed in the Act, to conserve endangered and threatened species, but this obligation is mostly ignored. If federal agencies did their job of helping to conserve imperiled and listed species, we would be much farther down the road to recovery for many of these species and their habitats.

Everyone knows the U.S. Fish and Wildlife Service and NOAA [National Oceanic and Atmospheric Administration] Fisheries are chronically underfunded to carry out their responsibilities under the Endangered Species Act. Interestingly, it wouldn't take much to change that. We're talking about a mere fraction of the money the government spends on roads, mines, timber hauls and other "habitat-busting" projects. Adequate funding would help address the listing backlog and backlog of species awaiting habitat designation, saving money in the long run by addressing situations before they're on the border of being too late. . . .

Supporters of the Endangered Species Act believe it is an important tool for protecting threatened animals, such as the bald eagle.

A Critical Law

Bottom line: The Endangered Species Act is one of our nation's most critical and essential environmental laws. Its basic premise and intent remain as sound today as when it was first crafted. And now, more than ever, our nation needs a strong Endangered Species Act.

The Endangered Species Act was passed to address a looming crisis of wildlife extinction that affects us all. It is simply naive to think we wouldn't revert to crisis mode absent a strong federal species protection law. And it is the height of ignorance to think, even for a minute, that weakening the Endangered Species Act wouldn't have dramatic and tangible consequences that would affect our entire ecosystem, and ultimately us.

When the nation rejoiced last month [April 2005] at the return of the ivory-billed woodpecker, Secretary [of the U.S. Department of the Interior Gale] Norton said that we rarely have a second chance to save wildlife from extinction. But the Endangered Species Act is all about *first* chances to do the same thing, about preventing wildlife extinction now, just in case nature is out of miracles.

EVALUATING THE AUTHORS' ARGUMENTS:

Jamie Rappaport Clark, the author of this viewpoint, and Richard W. Pombo, the author of the next viewpoint, offer different arguments on the effectiveness of the Endangered Species Act. After reading these viewpoints, can you think of any points these authors might agree on regarding endangered species?

The Endangered Species Act Does Not Work

Richard W. Pombo

"Success stories in species recovery due to the ESA are few and far between."

In the following viewpoint Richard W. Pombo states that the Endangered Species Act (ESA) does not protect endangered species in the United States. Since the act was signed in 1973, a large number of species have been listed, but very few have recovered, he maintains. According to Pombo, money and time that could be used to help recover species is being wasted on lawsuits filed under the act. In addition, he argues, the ESA leads to the abuse of private property owners and takes away their desire to protect endangered species. In 2005, Pombo was elected to his seventh term as a U.S. congressman representing California. He serves as chairman of the House Resources Committee and is a member of the House Agriculture Committee.

AS YOU READ, CONSIDER THE FOLLOWING QUESTIONS:
1. According to the author, of the 1,304 species listed under the ESA, how many have been recovered?

2. As explained by Pombo, how many people were displaced in order to protect the habitat of the longhorn elderberry bark beetle in California?
3. In the author's opinion, why is it inaccurate to judge the success of the ESA on how many species have avoided extinction?

The Endangered Species Act (ESA) was signed into law on December 28, 1973, by President Richard Milhous Nixon. *"Nothing is more priceless and more worthy of preservation than the rich array of animal life with which our country has been blessed,"* he said. *"It is a many-faceted treasure, of value to scholars, scientists, and nature lovers alike, and it forms a vital part of the heritage we all share as Americans."* . . .

Unfortunately, success stories in species recovery due to the ESA are few and far between. The law has fallen victim to unintended consequences, partisan politics, and counter-productive lawsuits filed by environmental organizations. These forces have rendered the ESA a "broken" law that is in desperate need of updating and modernizing after thirty years of failure. Congress has an obligation to address these unintended consequences and refocus the law's application on species recovery, its original intent.

An Abysmal Failure by the Numbers

The Endangered Species Act has become a program that checks species in for protection, conservation, and recovery, but never checks them out. According to the U.S. Fish and Wildlife Service (FWS), there are currently [in 2005] 1265 species in the United States that are listed under the ESA as threatened or endangered. An additional 39 species were listed and de-listed over the last thirty-two years, for a grand total of 1304 species in the Act's history.

Most Americans are surprised to learn that only *12 of these 1304 species* have been recovered in the Act's history, according to the Fish and Wildlife Service's data on de-listed species. *That is an abysmal, less than 1 percent rate of species recovery.* The FWS's statistics show that only 30 percent of species are "stable" and only 9 percent are "improving."

Few Success Stories

Moreover, numerous qualified studies assert that none of the species listed by the FWS to have been "recovered" in the United States may reasonably be claimed to have recovered as a result of the ESA. The fact is that the few recovery success stories are not even attributable to regulatory protections under the ESA, but unrelated factors such as bans on DDT and other [pesticides].

For example, in its 1997 report, *Conservation Under the Endangered Species Act, A Promise Broken,* the National Wilderness Institute (NWI) states that "there is no case which required the ESA to bring about the improvement of a species" and in at least four of the claimed recovery cases there was "little demonstrable change in the species' condition attributable to anything other than data error."

In short, the Endangered Species Act has failed to recover species, which was the intent of the law. . . .

Unintended Consequences

What was born of a desire to apply American ingenuity to the cause of saving species has become a tool not for species recovery, but for political, ideological, and fundraising goals.

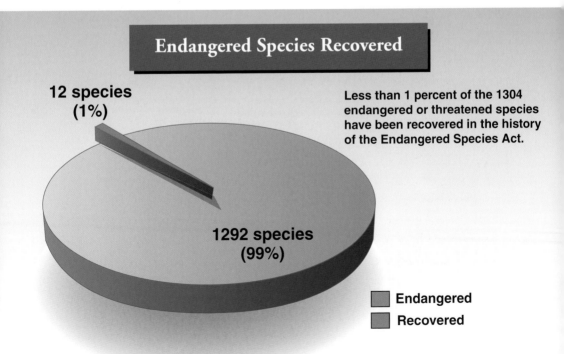

Endangered Species Recovered

12 species
(1%)

Less than 1 percent of the 1304 endangered or threatened species have been recovered in the history of the Endangered Species Act.

1292 species
(99%)

Endangered
Recovered

Source: Richard W. Pombo, Center for the Defense of Free Enterprise, 2005. www.cdfe.org.

Under the mantra of species protection, radical environmental organizations use the ESA to raise funds, block development projects, and prohibit legal land uses of nearly every kind. By filing inordinate numbers of lawsuits under the ESA, environmental organizations have hand-cuffed the FWS to courtroom defense tables, draining the time, money, and manpower Congress intended the service to spend on species recovery in the field.

According to the *Tulane University Environmental Law Journal,* "The entire ESA budget runs the risk of being consumed by the bottomless pit of litigation driven listings and designations. . . .

In yet another substantive analysis of ESA lawsuits filed by environmental organizations, the *Sacramento Bee* found that government biologists are being forced to spend more time on "legal chores" than on field work to recover species. The result? These organizations and their attorneys are collecting millions while species are ignored. Litigation involving the Endangered Species Act has become like

Former interior secretary Bruce Babbitt has blasted the Endangered Species Act as ineffectual because most of its budget is spent fighting legal battles.

"piecework" for these groups, as they seek attorney's fees and court awards from the federal government for the suits they file.

In fact, the flood of environmental litigation became so great that it bankrupted the Fish and Wildlife Service's fund for critical habitat in May of 2003. But this is certainly not new to the current [Bush] Administration. In a 2001 *New York Times* op-ed, former Secretary of the Interior Bruce Babbitt described the effects of environmental litigation thusly: "Struggling to keep up with these court orders, the Fish and Wildlife Service has diverted its best scientists and much of its budget for the Endangered Species Act away from more important tasks like evaluating candidates for listing and providing other protections for species on the brink of extinction." . . .

Shoot, Shovel, and Shut-Up

Another major unintended consequence of the ESA stems from the fact that it creates an adversarial relationship between government regulators and the people who are most critical to the goal of saving endangered species: America's farmers, ranchers, and private property owners. Known as the "shoot, shovel, and shut up" syndrome, research shows that the ESA has created perverse incentives that prompt land owners to actually destroy species habitat to rid their property of the liability that comes with endangered species.

This adversarial relationship and land-owner propensity to preemptively destroy species and their habitats is only perpetuated, if not exacerbated by management actions that are devoid of sound science and common sense.

Horror Stories and Government Abuse

In the recent case of the Klamath Basin and the endangered sucker fish, for example, it was determined that the sucker fish needed water supplies more than the area's farmers needed it to irrigate their crops and feed their families. The result was a devastating loss of family farms, human life and economic vitality. Only after the damage was done, the National Academy of Science (NAS) determined that [the] decision by the federal government to shut off irrigation water to nearly 1200 farmers and ranchers had "no sound scientific basis."

Or, consider the case of the endangered longhorn elderberry bark beetle and the Arboga levee in California. Weak levees went without repair because the work might have disturbed the habitat of the endangered beetle. The result: a huge flood broke the levee at the exact point where repairs were needed. Three human beings lost their lives. Approximately 500 homes, 9000 acres of prime farmland, and the four largest employers in the poorest county in the state were flooded. Overall, 35,000 people where displaced.

These and hundreds of other horror stories and cases of government abuse . . . under the ESA have fostered an adversarial relationship between government regulators and private property owners. This is incredibly deleterious to the goal of saving species because over 90% have habitat on private lands. . . .

Asay. © 2000 by Creators Syndicate. Reproduced by permission.

Updating and Strengthening the ESA

Many observers of the Endangered Species Act have gauged the law's performance on how many species are listed annually and have avoided extinction. However, merely preventing extinction is not a long-term measurable success, nor was it the intent of the law. The law was intended to conserve and *recover* America's endangered species. In that light, the Act has failed. It must be updated and strengthened to focus on results for species recovery or it will continue to be an unsustainable program that checks species in, but never checks them out.

EVALUATING THE AUTHORS' ARGUMENTS:

The author of this viewpoint believes that the Endangered Species Act is not an effective way to protect endangered species. How do you think Jamie Rappaport Clark, the author of the previous viewpoint, might respond to this argument?

Conservation Can Solve the West's Water Shortage

Philip L. Fradkin

"No wasteful civilization that outgrows its water resources ever survives."

As a result of drought and excessive consumption, the western United States is experiencing a severe and worsening water shortage, explains Philip L. Fradkin in the following viewpoint. Its communities cannot continue to live as if water is abundant, says Fradkin. He advises water conservation and sharing, warning that when water supplies are depleted, life cannot continue in that part of the country. Fradkin is the author of *Sagebrush Country: Land and the American West* and *Fallout: An American Nuclear Tragedy.*

AS YOU READ, CONSIDER THE FOLLOWING QUESTIONS:

1. According to the author, what is the status of Lake Powell?
2. What are the two major reasons for the West's water shortage, as explained by Fradkin?
3. How did water depletion impact the ancient Indians of the Southwest, according to the author?

With the five-year drought worsening in the Colorado River Basin, two Western icons are emerging like sore thumbs aching for attention. One is the casino-hotels of Las Vegas, [with] their resplendent fountains and the waterways on which gondolas float and water spurts in time to music. The other is the graceful arch of Glen Canyon Dam that backs up water in Lake Powell.

Both are distractions from root causes. The casino-hotels use mostly recycled water. The dam was a compromise that no one wanted to build in its present location but that everyone—federal dam builders, conservationists and basin states—agreed on. We are, despite the [conservationist] Ed Abbeys of the present day, stuck with it.

A wet weather cycle has given way to a prolonged dry cycle of unknown duration. The string of reservoirs along the Colorado River and its major tributaries—the Green, San Juan and Gila rivers—are shrinking to record low levels.

Water in Lake Mead is at a historic low level. A white ring around the edge of the lake shows how much the water level has receded over time.

Erratic Nature

Who really is to blame? The first is erratic Nature. In the spring of 1983, Lake Powell filled quickly. Boards and steel plates were used to raise the height of the dam, and the water came within six-thousandths of an inch of the top. Had the dam failed, direct ripple effects would have been felt past downstream Hoover Dam, all the way to the Gulf of California, while the indirect ones would have reached from Los Angeles to Denver, and beyond.

Now, the water level has shrunk to less than half the capacity of Lake Powell. Lake Mead behind Hoover Dam is also becoming a bathtub, complete with rings and scum in the bottom. There is talk of forceful measures imposed by federal fiat, which will only result in endless litigation and are not long-term solutions.

Human Consumption

The second problem is humans. We—you and I—use water in excessive amounts. We tend to think of the present as like the distant past.

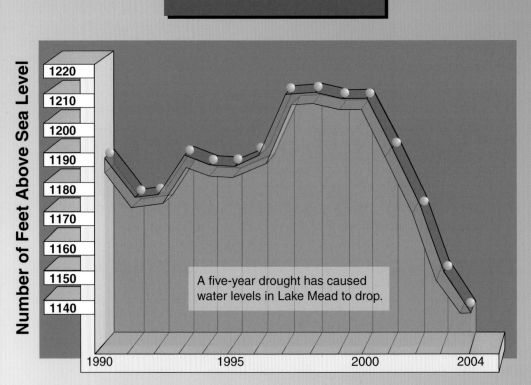

Lake Mead Water Levels

A five-year drought has caused water levels in Lake Mead to drop.

Number of Feet Above Sea Level

Source: U.S. Department of the Interior.

In 1922 seven western states signed an agreement to determine each state's right to water from the Colorado River.

That's what the seven Colorado River Basin states did when they unrealistically apportioned Colorado River water in 1922, based on wet years at the start of the last century.

We react, at best, with temporary solutions that tend to hurt others but not ourselves, then we drift, lazily, down the river again. We favor painless cures. My guess as to what is in the back of some people's minds now is to take water from agriculture and cut the flows to Mexico. It wasn't too long ago that a Los Angeles County supervisor suggested towing icebergs from the Arctic, or was it the Antarctic? I have read recently of ever more hare-brained schemes.

So what is a real solution? We could start over again with fresh thinking. Throw out the "Law of the River," that mishmash ranging from handshakes to international treaties to the 1922 compact. This myth of false abundance never did—and certainly no longer—fit realities of water in the West.

Sharing and Restraint

I have no idea what precisely can be substituted. I have only a few words of advice to offer: Share intelligently and fairly and with restraint.

People will be hurt, economically and socially. But the eventual price this oasis civilization will pay should make the prospect of some pain bearable for everyone. No wasteful civilization that outgrows its water resources ever survives in a form that even vaguely resembles its former wealth.

All we have to do is look at the fate of the ancient Indians of the Southwest who disappeared, or the empire of Mesopotamia in the Middle East, where soldiers are now fighting in what was once the Garden of Eden.

Twenty-three years ago I wrote a book titled *A River No More: The Colorado River and the West.* It concluded: "Certainly, the region, as symbolized by the Colorado River and the lands it succors, was approaching a new era in which the ultimate limits of what has always been considered a limitless frontier were in sight. Within a few more years, perhaps 20 or so, there was not going to be enough water to fulfill everybody's desires. The river was running dry."

Fifteen years later, in 1996, I wrote in the preface to a new edition of the book: "What occurred during the intervening years was a microcosm of the historic, long-term cycle of floods and droughts. The extremes illustrated how fragile the hold was on the water that sustained the Western states."

There is a race to see what we deplete first, water or oil. There is no substitute for water.

EVALUATING THE AUTHORS' ARGUMENTS:

The author of this viewpoint, Philip L. Fradkin, and the author of the next viewpoint, the Natural Resources Defense Council, both write essays on the West's water issues. On what points do you think they would agree? Where do you think they would differ?

Reducing Global Warming Can Solve the West's Water Shortage

"The . . . impacts of global warming in the West could be catastrophic."

Natural Resources Defense Council

In the following viewpoint the Natural Resources Defense Council (NRDC) insists that global warming will dramatically decrease water supplies in the western United States. As a result, says the NRDC, the economy and public health in this part of the country will suffer. The organization advocates immediate actions to reduce the advance of global warming. NRDC is a national environmental action organization that works to improve the state of America's environment.

AS YOU READ, CONSIDER THE FOLLOWING QUESTIONS:

1. By how much has the western climate warmed in the past fifty years, according to the author?
2. As explained by NRDC, what acts as temporary water storage in the western United States?
3. According to the author, by how much might hydropower output decrease in the Colorado River Basin as a result of global warming?

Global average temperatures have increased by 1.1 degrees Fahrenheit over the last century—warming faster than any time in the last 1000 years. The vast majority of mainstream scientists agree that these rising temperatures are caused by carbon dioxide and other heat-trapping gases produced from the burning of fossil fuels in cars and power plants.

The arid American West appears to be particularly susceptible to the effects of global warming. Over the past 50 years, the western climate has warmed on average by 1.4 degrees Fahrenheit, and climate models predict a further increase of 3.6 to 12.6 degrees Fahrenheit in the West by the end of the century. A growing body of scientific evidence is linking global warming trends with changes in precipitation, declining snowpack, and smaller and earlier spring runoff—conditions that determine the quantity and timing of water supplies in the West, as well as wildfire risk. Many parts of the West are already experiencing devastating multi-year droughts. If current global warming trends continue, they present serious consequences to many bedrock elements of western life, from agriculture and ranching to skiing, tourism, biodiversity and public health.

Many scientists believe that the emissions of vehicles on America's highways contribute to global warming, which could be responsible for droughts in the West.

One of the concerns about global warming is that it could reduce snowpack in the West, which would in turn decrease water supply.

Without taking immediate steps to reduce global warming pollution, the economic, hydrologic and environmental impacts of global warming in the West could be catastrophic.

Decreased Water Supplies

Global warming may not only be exacerbating the current drought in much of the West, but may cause similar drought-like conditions in the future. Snowpack, which acts as temporary water storage, provides up to 75 percent of the region's annual water supply. Additional increases in global temperatures will decrease snowpack in the West by as much as 40 percent by 2060. The loss of snowpack will decrease the total water supply both locally and regionally, making summers drier and droughts worse. Further reduced water supplies will exacerbate existing conflicts as well as generate new urban, agricultural and natural resource–related problems.

A rise in temperatures could negatively affect many crops grown in the American West, such as this soybean crop.

In the Colorado River Basin, for example, high elevation snow pack contributes approximately 70 percent of the annual runoff. With global warming predicted to result in an estimated 24 percent decrease in snowpack over the next 35 years, the current drought conditions in the Southwest could become the norm. The largest impacts may be felt in the Upper Basin states of Wyoming, Utah, Colorado and New Mexico, as the Colorado River Compact prioritizes the delivery of water to the Lower Basin states of Arizona, California and Nevada. However, it is estimated that with increased global warming the compact requirements may only be met 59 to 75 percent of the time.

In California, global warming puts the drinking water supply for 22 million people at risk. Every year, a delicate balance must be maintained in the San Francisco Bay–Delta Estuary between fresh water inflows from Sierra Nevada rivers and salt water intrusion from the Pacific Ocean. Decreased river flows resulting from reduced snow packs and earlier snow melts may result in higher spring-summer salinities in the Delta. The frail levee system throughout the Delta is already vulnerable to failures, which could produce massive inflows of salty sea water and taint water supplies. Without action, the risk to California's primary water supply will increase as sea levels continue to rise by as much as 2 to 3 feet over the next 100 years.

Decreased Hydropower Production

Reduced snowpack and early snowmelt runoff will also reduce hydropower production. Studies have shown that a 10 percent decrease in flows can result in a 36 percent reduction in power production. Within the Columbia River Basin, projected reductions in snowpack runoff combined with meeting other water demands could reduce hydropower production by as much as 20 percent by 2060. In the Colorado River Basin, decreased river runoff could reduce hydropower output by 50 percent. In streams throughout California's Sierra Nevada, spring runoff is occurring as much as three weeks earlier than in 1948. Early snowmelt exacerbates the problem by reducing the flows that would normally be available later in the spring and summer, when electricity demand is greater. . . .

Reduced Agricultural Production

Decreased crop yields and reduced water supplies resulting from global warming have the potential to seriously affect the local and regional agricultural economies in the West. Studies in the last year [2004] have concluded that increasing temperatures negatively affected crop yields for rice, soybeans and corn. The Intergovernmental Panel on Climate Change states that global warming may cause corn yields to drop by 15 to 30 percent across the United States. Similarly, the U.S. Environmental Protection Agency (EPA) estimates that as temperatures near the upper tolerance levels for wheat, crop yields will drop 10 to 30 percent in New Mexico and Utah, approximately 48 to 66 percent in California, and up to 70 percent in Arizona. . . .

Unchecked, global warming will harm the economy, public health and environment in the Western states.

> ### EVALUATING THE AUTHOR'S ARGUMENTS:
>
> List three different pieces of evidence that the Natural Resources Defense Council uses to support its argument that reducing global warming can help solve the West's water shortage. Which of these do you find the most convincing? Why?

Drilling in the Arctic Refuge Will Harm the Environment

Defenders of Wildlife

"Oil development would have a severe, detrimental impact on wildlife populations in the Arctic National Wildlife Refuge."

Alaska's Arctic National Wildlife Refuge (ANWR) is a refuge located in northeastern Alaska. While it is home to a great variety of wildlife, the area is also believed to contain large oil reserves. Since the early 1990s there have been numerous unsuccessful attempts to get permission to drill for oil there. In the following viewpoint Defenders of Wildlife warns that drilling in ANWR would severely harm wildlife populations. According to the organization, conservation and the use of renewable fuels is a better alternative to the destruction of this wilderness. Defenders of Wildlife is a conservation group dedicated to the protection of native wild animals and plants in their natural communities.

AS YOU READ, CONSIDER THE FOLLOWING QUESTIONS:
1. How many species of birds find breeding, nesting, or resting places in the refuge, according to the authors?
2. As cited by Defenders of Wildlife, how many contaminated waste sites are associated with oil development in Prudhoe Bay?
3. In the authors' opinion, how might wintertime seismic exploration impact polar bears?

The United States government set aside [the Arctic National Wildlife Refuge] for protection more than 40 years ago under the presidency of Dwight Eisenhower to protect its "unique wildlife, wilderness and recreation values." In 1980, President [Jimmy] Carter signed the Alaska National Interest Lands Conservation Act, or ANILCA, which doubled the size of the Arctic Range and renamed it the Arctic National Wildlife Refuge. This law closed the 1.5 million acres of the refuge's coastal plain to gas and oil exploration unless specifically authorized by Congress.

Oil companies and their pro-drilling advocates in Congress and the White House are determined to secure drilling authorization in the 109th Congress. Defenders of Wildlife is determined to stop them.

The Refuge's Coastal Plain

The 1.5 million acre coastal plain, the biological heart of the Arctic National Wildlife Refuge, is home to the full range of arctic and subarctic life. Over 130 bird species, including those that visit each of the lower 48 states, find breeding, nesting or resting places on the plain. It is the most important on-shore denning area in the United States for polar bears. The coastal plain is also the principal calving ground of the 130,000-strong Porcupine caribou herd, which has made its annual migration to the plain for tens of thousands of years. The caribou herd is a resource shared with Canada, the second largest herd in the United States, and a key source of food, clothing and medicine for the Gwich'in Indians. Grizzly bears, wolves, arctic foxes, whales and other species also thrive in the region.

The Arctic National Wildlife Refuge provides important natural resources for the Gwich'in Indians. Here, a Gwich'in boy holds up pictures he drew of the caribou, asking that ANWR not be opened for oil drilling.

Impact of Oil Drilling

Coastal plain oil development would require a spider's web of industrial complexes across virtually the entire plain—hundreds of miles of roads and feeder pipelines, refineries, living quarters for hundreds of workers, landfills, water reservoirs, docks and gravel causeways, production plants, gas processing facilities, seawater treatment plants, power plants and gravel mines. And the oil development process is rife with catastrophe. At the Prudhoe Bay oilfield just west of the Arctic Refuge, spills of oil products and hazardous substances happen *every single day,* and noise and air pollution are rampant. According to Alaska's Department of Environmental Conservation, there are 55 contaminated waste sites already associated with this development.

Oil and Wildlife Don't Mix

The threats to wildlife would be enormous. In a letter to President [George W.] Bush, over 1000 scientists and natural resource managers from the U.S. and Canada confirmed that oil development could significantly disrupt the fragile ecosystem of the coastal plain and seriously harm caribou, polar bears, muskoxen, snow geese and other wildlife. Biologists project that the birthrate of the Porcupine caribou may fall by 40 percent if drilling is allowed. Wintertime seismic exploration could cause polar bears to abandon their dens, leaving their cubs to die. Wolves and grizzly bears that prey on newborn caribou would also be adversely affected by the impacts of oil drilling, and the more than 130 species of migratory birds that depend on the refuge's coastal plain would suffer permanent habitat losses from oil development. Simply put, oil development would have a severe, detrimental impact on wildlife populations in the Arctic National Wildlife Refuge.

Arctic Oil Is Not the Answer—Now or in the Future

No oil or natural gas would flow from the Refuge for at least ten years. The amount of oil that the U.S. Geological Survey estimates could

Caribou are one of many creatures that make their home in the Arctic National Wildlife Refuge.

Opinions on Drilling

Washington Post polls show that more people now favor oil drilling in the Arctic National Wildlife Refuge than they did sixteen years ago.

	Yes	No	No opinion
6/5/05	48	49	4
4/21/02	43	50	7
1/27/02	48	48	4
4/22/01	41	55	4
1/15/01	38	56	5
5/13/89	26	60	13

Source: *Washington Post*–ABC News, 2005.

be economically recovered from the Arctic Refuge would amount to only a few months' supply for America. Expanded conservation, greater use of the renewable energy, and alternative fuels can save far more than what might lie beneath the Arctic Refuge. For example, a modest increase in the fuel economy of cars and light trucks of about 2 miles per gallon would save more than a million barrels a day—far more than is likely to be underneath the Arctic Refuge.

EVALUATING THE AUTHORS' ARGUMENTS:

In this viewpoint the author believes that drilling for oil in the Arctic Refuge will devastate wildlife there. The author of the next viewpoint disagrees. After reading both viewpoints, what is your opinion about drilling in the Arctic Refuge? Cite from the text to support your answer.

Drilling in the Arctic Refuge Will Not Harm the Environment

"Advanced technology . . . [assures] that the Arctic environment and its wildlife will be protected."

Gale A. Norton

Since the early 1990s there have been numerous unsuccessful attempts to get permission to drill for oil in Alaska's Arctic National Wildlife Refuge, which is believed to contain large oil reserves. In the following viewpoint Gale A. Norton argues that drilling should be authorized because it will provide much-needed energy for Americans. In addition, she maintains, new technology will allow drilling to take place without harming the natural habitat or the wildlife living in this area. Norton was sworn in as the forty-eighth secretary of the U.S. Department of the Interior in January 2001.

AS YOU READ, CONSIDER THE FOLLOWING QUESTIONS:
1. As explained by Norton, why did past Arctic oil development often scar the land?
2. According to the author, why does Arctic exploration today only occur in the frozen winter?
3. In Norton's opinion, if development is allowed in the 1002 area, how small will the "footprint" of equipment and facilities be?

E ven though it is noon, the landscape is pitch black. The wind chill stands at 70 below zero. A lone man drives across a vast frozen plain on a road made of ice. He sits atop a large, bug-like machine with enormous wheels. He is heading for a spot on the tundra pinpointed by satellite imagery to explore for oil. When the spring thaw comes and the road melts, any evidence that a man or a machine ever crossed there will be gone.

Changes in Oil Exploration

This is the world of Arctic energy exploration in the 21st century. It is as different from what oil exploration used to be as the compact supercomputers of today are different from the huge vacuum tube computers of the 1950s. Through the use of advanced technology, we have learned not only to get access to oil and gas reserves in Arctic environments but also to protect their ecosystems and wildlife.

Technological advances in oil exploration are at the heart of a debate over America's energy future. Congress will soon decide whether to

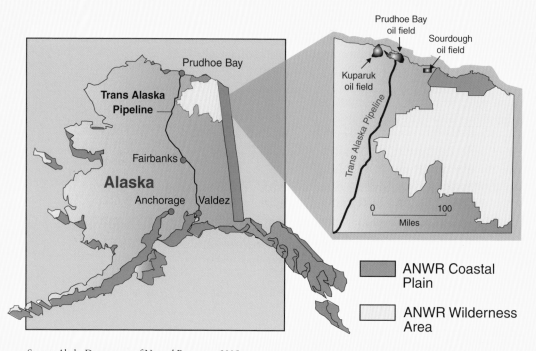

The Arctic National Wildlife Refuge (ANWR)

Source: Alaska Department of Natural Resources, 2005.

Drilling for oil in Alaska's Arctic National Wildlife Refuge has been a subject of controversy for decades.

open up a sliver of the Arctic National Wildlife Refuge—called the 1002 area—to energy development.[1] Opponents will pretend that new, less invasive technology doesn't exist. It is important for Americans to understand that it does, and that it works.

In past decades, Arctic oil development involved huge amounts of equipment that had to be moved over gravel roads and laid upon large gravel pads. The machines that transported this equipment often scarred the land, especially in spring and summer.

1. The 1002 area is located along the coastal plain of the Arctic National Wildlife Refuge. As of this writing, oil exploration was being debated in Congress.

New Technology

American ingenuity has tackled this problem. Today, oil exploration in the Arctic occurs only in the frozen winter. Workers build roads and platforms of ice to protect the soil and vegetation. Trucks with huge tires called rolligons distribute load weights over large areas of snow to minimize the impact on the tundra below.

Meanwhile, innovations in platform development and directional drilling mean that we need fewer and smaller pads to tap into oil and gas reserves. From a single platform, we can explore an underground area nearly the size of the District of Columbia.

Likewise, satellite infrared imaging helps energy companies to avoid key wildlife habitat and environmentally sensitive areas while 3-D seismic data imaging improves the chances of drilling a successful well by 50 percent, meaning fewer wells.

Substantial Oil Reserves

In 1980, when Congress created the refuge, it set aside the 1002 area for possible future energy development. To date, Congress has not approved this development because of environmental concerns. In the meantime, America's domestic production of energy has declined and we have become more and more dependent on imported oil.

As part of a comprehensive energy strategy of promoting conservation and reducing dependence on foreign oil, we must increase our energy production here at home. The 1002 area is potentially the largest untapped source of oil and gas on American soil. While we cannot promise that there will be no impact on the wildlife and habitat of the 1002 area, we can promise no significant impact.

Strict Standards of Protection

In fact, legislation to open up the area passed [in 2004] by the House of Representatives laid down the strictest environmental standards ever applied to energy development and flatly stated that development must "result in no significant adverse effect on fish and wildlife, their habitat, subsistence resources, and the environment."

We can meet this standard because of the extraordinary advances in oil field technology. If approved by Congress, the overall "footprint" of the equipment and facilities needed to develop the 1002 area would be restricted to 2,000 acres, an area about the size of a regional airport in a refuge the size of South Carolina.

With this advanced technology and the strict requirements of the legislation, the American people will have access to much needed energy to heat our homes and run our businesses while being assured that the Arctic environment and its wildlife will be protected.

Glossary

carbon dioxide (CO$_2$): A gas that occurs naturally in the atmosphere and is also produced by decaying matter or when fossil fuels are burned.

Clean Air Act: A series of regulations in the United States that have the purpose of diminishing air pollution.

critical habitat: The areas of land, water, and airspace that a species needs for survival. Critical habitat is protected under the Endangered Species Act of 1973.

delisting: Removing plants and animals protected under the Endangered Species Act from the official list of threatened or endangered species, usually because the species have recovered or have become extinct.

ecosystem: All living things as well as the soil, air, and water within a habitat.

endangered species: A species that has so few members that it is in danger of becoming extinct.

EPA: The Environmental Protection Agency, authorized by Congress in 1970. It enforces environmental protection laws in the United States.

extinction: Ceasing to exist.

fossil fuels: Crude oil, coal, and natural gas formed from the decaying remains of ancient organisms.

global warming: An increase in the average global temperature over a period of time.

greenhouse effect: The natural process whereby atmospheric gases act like the glass in a greenhouse, letting the sun's energy in and trapping some of it to warm the planet.

greenhouse gases: Gases that easily absorb heat and create the greenhouse effect; these gases include ozone and carbon dioxide.

habitat: The place that provides everything that a plant or animal needs to live and grow.

listing: Adding a species to the official U.S. government list of endangered or threatened species according to the provisions of the Endangered Species Act. Listed species are entitled to the full protection of the government.

native species: Species that occur naturally in an area and have not been imported by people.

oil reserves: The amount of oil that is estimated to be available for extraction from a particular site.

refuge: A place where species of plants and animals are protected from human activity.

smog: A combination of the words *smoke* and *fog,* used to describe polluted air.

species: A group of plants or animals of the same kind that produce young like themselves.

Facts About the Environment

Ecosystem Change

- Over the past fifty years humans have changed ecosystems faster and more extensively than in any period in human history.
- According to the World Wildlife Federation, in 2001 humanity's use of natural resources exceeded Earth's biological capacity by 20 percent.
- Nearly 78 million people are currently added to the world's population each year.
- Five percent of the world's population live in the United States, but Americans produce 50 percent of the world's waste.

Extinction

- Although the extinction of various species is a natural phenomenon, the rate of extinction occurring in today's world is exceptional—estimates range from one hundred to one thousand times greater than normal.
- In the United States 389 species of animals and 599 species of plants are currently listed as threatened or endangered.
- According to a report by the Center for Biological Diversity, 108 animals and plants are known to have become extinct in the United States since the creation of the Endangered Species Act in 1973.

Freshwater

- Less than 1 percent of the water on Earth is freshwater.
- According to the conservation group Environmental Literacy, nearly half a billion people around the world face freshwater shortages. That number is expected to grow to 2.8 billion by 2025.
- In the United States the Environmental Protection Agency estimates that pesticides contaminate the groundwater in thirty-eight states, polluting the primary source of drinking water for more than half the country's population.

Oceans

- Approximately 70 percent of the planet's surface is covered by ocean.

- According to the Canadian Department of Fisheries and Oceans, plastic trash is now considered to be as dangerous to marine organisms as oil spills, toxic wastes, and heavy metals.

- The United Nations Food and Agriculture Organization estimates that 27 million tons of fish are discarded every year as unwanted because they are either species of low commercial value or juveniles that cannot be kept legally.

- According to the Pew Oceans Commission, at least a third of U.S. fish stocks are currently being overfished.

- The Nature Conservancy believes that coral reefs are currently one of the most endangered ecosystems on the planet. The organization estimates that if the present rate of reef destruction continues, 70 percent of the world's coral reefs will be destroyed within our lifetime.

Air

- Burning 1 gallon (3.8l) of gasoline generates 20 pounds (9kg) of carbon dioxide. According to the U.S. Department of Transportation, the average car commuter generates about 7,350 tons (6,668 t) of carbon dioxide a year.

- According to the Foundation for Clean Air Progress, it would take twenty of today's new cars to generate the same amount of air pollution as one mid-1960s-model car.

- Smog levels were measured in twenty-eight national parks from 1993 to 2002. At twenty of these national parks, smog levels increased over the ten-year period. Improvements were seen in six parks.

- Estimates of the annual human health costs of outdoor air pollution range from $14 billion to $55 billion annually.

- According to the Foundation for Clean Air Progress, since 1970 Americans have cut releases of air pollutants by more than 50 million tons (45 million t).

- According to the American Lung Association, air pollution is responsible for seventy thousand deaths each year in the United States.

Forests

- The world's forests help determine global temperature, maintain ecological diversity, and protect soil from erosion.

- It is estimated that at the beginning of European settlement in 1630, the area of forestland that would become the United States was 1 billion acres (423 million ha) or about 46 percent of the total land area. By 1907 the area of forestland had declined to an estimated 758 million acres (307 million ha) or 34 percent of the total land area. In 1997, 746 million acres (302 million ha)—or 33 percent of the total land area of the United States—was in forestland.

- After intensive logging in the late nineteenth century and early to mid-twentieth century, 55 percent of the forests on the nation's timberland is less than 50 years old. Six percent of the nation's timberland is more than 175 years old.

Organizations to Contact

American Council on Science and Health (ACSH)
1995 Broadway, 2nd Fl., New York, NY 10023-5860
(212) 362-7044
fax: (212) 362-4919
e-mail: acsh@acsh.org
Web site: www.acsh.org

ACSH is a consumer education consortium concerned with environmental and health-related issues. The council publishes the quarterly *Priorities*, position papers such as "Global Climate Change and Human Health," and numerous reports, including "Arsenic, Drinking Water, and Health" and "The DDT Ban Turns 30."

Canadian Centre for Pollution Prevention (C2P2)
100 Charlotte St., Sarnia, ON N7T 4R2 Canada
(800) 667-9790
fax: (519) 337-3486
e-mail: info@c2p2online.com
Web site: www.c2p2online.com

The Canadian Centre for Pollution Prevention is Canada's leading resource on ways to end pollution. It provides access to national and international information on pollution and prevention, online forums, and publications, including *Practical Pollution Training Guide* and the newsletter *At the Source*, which C2P2 publishes three times a year.

Cato Institute
1000 Massachusetts Ave. NW, Washington, DC 20001-5403
(202) 842-0200
fax: (202) 842-3490
e-mail: cato@cato.org
Web site: www.cato.org

The Cato Institute is a libertarian public policy research foundation that aims to limit the role of government and protect civil liberties. The institute believes EPA regulations are too stringent. Publications offered on its Web site include the bimonthly *Cato Policy Report,* the quarterly journal *Regulation,* and numerous books and articles.

Competitive Enterprise Institute (CEI)
1001 Connecticut Ave. NW, Suite 1250, Washington, DC 20036
(202) 331-1010
fax: (202) 331-0640
e-mail: info@cei.org
Web site: www.cei.org

CEI is a nonprofit public policy organization dedicated to the principles of free enterprise and limited government. The institute believes private incentives and property rights, rather than government regulations, are the best way to protect the environment. CEI's publications include the newsletter *Monthly Planet, On Point* policy briefs, and the book *True State of the Planet.*

Environmental Protection Agency (EPA)
Ariel Rios Bldg., 1200 Pennsylvania Ave. NW, Washington, DC 20460
(202) 272-0167
Web site: www.epa.gov

The EPA is the federal agency in charge of protecting the environment and controlling pollution. The agency works toward these goals by enacting and enforcing regulations, identifying and fining polluters, assisting local businesses and local environmental agencies, and cleaning up polluted sites. The EPA publishes periodic reports and the monthly *EPA Activities Update.*

Environment Canada
351 St. Joseph Blvd., Gratineau, QC K1A OH3 Canada
(819) 997-2800
fax: (819) 953-2225
e-mail: enviroinfo@ec.gc.ca
Web site: www.ec.gc.ca

Environment Canada is a department of the Canadian government. Its goal is the achievement of sustainable development in Canada through conservation and environmental protection. The department publishes reports, including "Environmental Signals 2003," and fact sheets on a number of topics, such as pollution prevention.

Foundation for Clean Air Progress (FCAP)
1801 K St. NW, Suite 1000L, Washington, DC 20036
(800) 272-1604
e-mail: info@cleanairprogress.org
Web site: www.cleanairprogress.org

FCAP is a nonprofit organization that believes the public is unaware of the progress that has been made in reducing air pollution. The foundation represents various sectors of business and industry in providing information to the public about improving air quality trends. FCAP publishes reports and studies demonstrating that air pollution is on the decline, including *Breathing Easier About Energy—a Healthy Economy and Healthier Air* and *Study on Air Quality Trends, 1970–2015.*

Global Warming International Center (GWIC)
22W381 Seventy-fifth St., Naperville, IL 60565
(630) 910-1551
fax: (630) 910-1562
Web site: www.globalwarming.net

GWIC is an international body that provides information on global warming science and policy to industries and governmental and non-governmental organizations. The center sponsors research supporting the understanding of global warming and ways to reduce the problem. It publishes the quarterly newsletter *World Resource Review.*

Hudson Institute
Herman Kahn Center
5395 Emerson Way, PO Box 26-919, Indianapolis, IN 46226
(317) 545-1000
fax: (317) 545-1384
e-mail: johnmc@hii.hudson.org
Web site: www.hudson.org

The Hudson Institute is a public policy research center whose members are elected from academia, government, and industry. The institute promotes the power of the free market and human ingenuity to solve environmental problems. Its publications include the monthly *Outlook* and the monthly policy bulletin *Foresight.*

Natural Resources Defense Council (NRDC)
40 W. Twentieth St., New York, NY 10011
(212) 727-2700
(212) 727-1773
e-mail: nrdcinfo@nrdc.org
Web site: www.nrdc.org

The NRDC is a nonprofit organization with more than four hundred thousand members. It uses laws and science to protect the environment, including wildlife and wild places. NRDC publishes the quarterly magazine *OnEarth* and hundreds of reports, including "Development and Dollars," and the annual report "Testing the Waters."

Pew Center on Global Climate Change
2101 Wilson Blvd., Suite 550, Arlington, VA 22201
(703) 516-4146
fax: (703) 841-1422
Web site: www.pewclimate.org

The Pew Center on Global Climate Change is a nonpartisan organization dedicated to educating the public and policy makers about the causes and potential consequences of global climate change and informing them of ways to reduce the emissions of greenhouse gases. Its reports include "Designing a Climate-Friendly Energy Policy" and "The Science of Climate Change."

Political Economy Research Center (PERC)
502 S. Nineteenth Ave., Bozeman, MT 59718
(406) 587-9591
e-mail: perc@perc.org
Web site: www.perc.org

PERC is a research and educational foundation that focuses primarily on environmental and natural resource issues. Its approach emphasizes the use of the free markets and the importance of private property rights in protecting the environment. Publications include *PERC Viewpoint* and *PERC Reports.*

Sierra Club
85 Second St., 2nd Fl., San Francisco, CA 94105
(415) 977-5500

fax: (415) 977-5799
e-mail: information@sierraclub.org
Website: www.sierraclub.org

The Sierra Club is a grassroots organization with chapters in every state that promotes the protection and conservation of natural resources. The organization maintains separate committees on air quality, global environment, and solid waste, among other environmental concerns, to help achieve its goals. It publishes books, fact sheets, the bimonthly magazine *Sierra,* and the *Planet* newsletter, which appears several times a year.

Worldwatch Institute
1776 Massachusetts Ave. NW, Washington, DC 20036-1904
(202) 452-1999
fax: (202) 296-7365
e-mail: worldwatch@worldwatch.org
Web site: www.worldwatch.org

Worldwatch is a nonprofit public policy research organization dedicated to informing the public and policy makers about emerging problems and trends and the complex links between the environment and the economy. Its publications include *Vital Signs,* issued every year, the bimonthly magazine *World Watch,* the Environmental Alert series, and numerous policy papers, including "Unnatural Disasters," and "City Limits: Putting the Brakes on Sprawl."

For Further Reading

Books

Brennan, Scott R., Jay H. Withgott, and Jay Withgott, *Environment: The Science Behind the Stories.* Boston: Benjamin Cummings, 2004. Uses case studies and real data to demonstrate the role of science in identifying and solving environmental problems.

Day, Kristen A., ed., *China's Environment and the Challenge of Sustainable Development.* Armonk, NY: M.E. Sharpe, 2005. A collection of essays that examine the impact of economic growth on China's environment and the challenge of achieving sustainable development there.

Ellis, Richard, *The Empty Ocean.* Washington, DC: Shearwater, 2004. Presents stories and historical and scientific data about human use and abuse of the sea and the effect these actions have had on sea life.

Glantz, Michael H., *Climate Affairs: A Primer.* Washington, DC: Island, 2003. Draws on a range of study areas—including climate science, politics, policy and law, economics, and ethics—to explore the many dimensions of the effects of climate change.

Kennedy Jr., Robert F., *Crimes Against Nature: How George W. Bush and His Corporate Pals Are Plundering the Country and Hijacking Our Democracy.* New York: HarperCollins, 2004. An environmental attorney charges that the administration has eviscerated the laws that have protected the nation's air, water, public lands, and wildlife.

Langholz, Jeffrey, and Kelly Turner, *You Can Prevent Global Warming: 51 Easy Ways.* Kansas City, MO: Andrews McMeel, 2003. Presents suggestions of hundreds of simple things that can be done by citizens to help minimize global warming.

Lesinger, Klaus M., Karen Schmitt, and Rajul Pandya-Lorch, *Six Billion and Counting: Population Growth and Food Security in the 21st Century.* Washington, DC: International Food Policy Research Institute, 2002. Describes the effects of rapid population growth on social and economic conditions and on natural resources and considers what population growth will mean for the world's food supply.

Parks, Peggy J., *Global Resources*. Farmington Hills, MI: Lucent, 2004. Examines the question of whether Earth's natural resources are being depleted. Discusses issues that affect the planet's oceans, freshwater, minerals, forests, and fossil fuels.

Slobodkin, Lawrence B., *A Citizen's Guide to Ecology*. New York: Oxford University Press, 2003. Examines the science behind claims about environmental crisis in species extinction, population growth, global warming, and other environmental topics.

Speth, James Gustave, *Red Sky at Morning: America and the Crisis of the Global Environment*. New Haven, CT: Yale University Press, 2004. The dean of the Yale University School of Forestry and Environmental Studies warns about the seriousness of the global environmental crisis, stressing that current environmental trends cannot continue.

Periodicals

Anderson, Terry L., "Cooling the Global Warming Debate," *Hoover Digest,* Summer 2004.

Bandow, Doug, "Endangered Species Endanger Landowners' Rights," *Conservative Chronicle,* February 25, 2004.

Barnes, Peter, "Sharing the Wealth of the Commons," *Dollars & Sense,* November/December 2004.

Bollier, David, "Who Owns the Sky? Reviving the Commons," *In These Times,* March 29, 2004.

Burdick, Alan, "When Nature Assaults Itself," *New York Times,* April 22, 2003.

Carrasquillo, Nelson, "Environmentalists Should Worry About *All* the Children," *Progressive Populist,* April 15, 2004.

Hillesland, Marya, "Creating Policies That Promote a Healthy Society," *Friends Journal,* October 2004.

Jackson, Derrick Z., "Neglecting Mother Earth," *Liberal Opinion Week,* February 14, 2005.

James, Sarah, "We Are the Ones Who Have Everything to Lose," *Wild Earth,* Winter 2003/2004.

Johnson, Geoffrey, "'Greenwashing' Leaves a Stain of Distortion," *Los Angeles Times,* August 22, 2004.

Johnson, Paul, "Pay No Attention to the Scientific Pontiffs," *Spectator,* January 17, 2004.

Kristof, Nicholas D., "Nukes Are Green," *New York Times,* April 9, 2005.

Leavitt, David I., "It's the Environment, Stupid," *Dissent,* Spring 2004.

McEwan, Ian, "The Hot Breath of Civilization," *Los Angeles Times,* April 22, 2005.

McGrath, Susan, "Attack of the Alien Invaders," *National Geographic,* March 2005.

Multinational Monitor, "A Sea Change to Reverse the Oceans Crisis," September 2003.

Myers, Nancy, "The Rise of the Precautionary Principle," *Multinational Monitor,* September 2004.

Nader, Ralph, "U.S. Ignores Environmental Threats," *Progressive Populist,* November 1, 2004.

Nelson, Robert H., "Suppose the Globe *Is* Warming," *Liberty,* February 2003.

Nowicki, Brian, "Delays in Endangered Species Act Protections Lead to Extinctions," *Earth Island Journal,* Autumn 2004.

Schwartz, Joel, "Clearing the Air," *Regulation,* Summer 2003.

Simmons, Daniel R., and Randy T. Simmons, "The Endangered Species Act Turns 30," *Regulation,* Winter 2003/2004.

Singleton, Elizabeth, "Overcoming Government Obstacles," *PERC Reports,* June 2004.

Will, George, "Global Warming Crowd Creates State of Fear," *Conservative Chronicle,* December 29, 2004.

Web Sites

Climate Solutions (http://climatesolutions.org). Provides basic information on global warming as well as resources and links to other global warming sites.

National Library for the Environment (www.ncseonline.org). This site brings together information and resources on a large variety of environmental topics.

Negative Population Growth (http://npg.org). Contains numerous articles discussing the detrimental effects of overpopulation on the environment and on quality of life.

Rainforest Alliance (www.rainforest-alliance.org). This site offers fact sheets and research papers about sustainable living and the preservation of biodiversity, as well as links to other conservation Web sites.

SeaWeb (www.seaweb.org). Offers oceans news and events, educational material, and links to oceans-related sites.

World Environmental Organization (www.world.org). Provides information on the environment, as well as numerous links to other environmental Web sites.

World Resources Institute (www.wri.org). Offers environmental news, educational material, links to environment-related sites, and global environment information.

Index

Picture Credits

Cover: © Gary Braasch/CORBIS
Maury Aaseng, 25, 30, 41, 72, 79, 80, 85, 104, 106
© age fotostock/SuperStock, 47, 71
Thorkild Amdi/EPA/Landov, 34
© James L. Amos/SuperStock, 49
AP/Wide World Photos, 21, 52, 55, 81, 86
© Peter Beck/CORBIS, 98
© Ralph A. Clevenger/CORBIS, 22
© Corel Corporation, 35, 93
Digital Vision/Getty Images, 15, 58
Tamia Dowlatabadi, 92
© Natalie Fobes/CORBIS, 12, 61
© Chinch Gryniewicz/Ecoscene/CORBIS, 37
© Richard I'Anson/Lonely Planet Images, 11, 40
© Larry Lee Photography/CORBIS, 107
Claus Lunau/Bonnier Publications/Science Photo Library, 28
David McNew/Getty Images, 91
© Michael Newman/Photo Edit, 74
Photo courtesy of Rolligon Corporation, 106
PhotoDisc, 18, 33, 60, 67, 96
Photonica/Getty Images, 65
Photos.com, 10
Hazir Reka/Reuters/Landov, 42
© Chris Rogers/CORBIS, 97
© Joel W. Rogers/CORBIS, 103
Rickey Rogers/Reuters/Landov, 29
© Les Stone/Zuma/CORBIS, 76
© Bill Varie/CORBIS, 13
Scott Weiss, 48
Doug Wilson/Time Life Pictures/Getty Images, 102

About the Editor

Andrea C. Nakaya, a native of New Zealand, holds a BA in English and an MA in communication from San Diego State University. She has spent more than three years at Greenhaven Press, where she works as a full-time book editor. Andrea currently lives in Encinitas, California, with her husband Jamie and their daughter Natalie. In her free time she enjoys traveling, reading, gardening, waterskiing, and snowboarding.